CIVITATES ORBIS TERRARUM

CITIES OF THE WORLD

EUROPE - AFRICA - ASIA

Introduction
by
Lelio Pagani

MAGNA BOOKS

Original title: Civitates Orbis Terrarum
Città del mondo - Europa - Africa - Asie
© 1990 Orsa Maggiore SpA, Torriana (FO), Italy
© English edition published by
Magna Books, Magna Road, Wigston, Leicester,
LE 8 2ZH, England.
This edition translated by Simon Knight in
association with First Edition, Cambridge.
Graphics realization by Lucchetti Editore - Bergamo,
(Italy);
Printed by GEP - Cremona, (Italy);
All rights reserved.
ISBN 1 85422 113 2

The scholar chiefly responsible for preparing the *Civitates* for publication was Georg Braun. In his learned preface, after dwelling on the quality of the draughtsmanship and the artists' skill in capturing the spirit of the different cities, he goes on to discuss the purpose of the work, maintaining that as well as giving great pleasure to mind and eye it has an immediate practical application.

He first commends the experience of travelling, which more than any other takes the traveller out of his familiar surroundings and brings him into direct contact with other peoples and places. By travelling, he says:

> diversarium gentium ritus, disciplinae, leges, mores, instituta et consuetudines multo accuratius intelliguntur, quam si ea, quae numquam vidimus, sola historica lectione tracteremus[1].

But not all have the opportunity to travel. There are difficulties of many kinds, and dangers lie in the way of those who would venture abroad:

> per varias partes oberrare, multasque urbes, oppida peragrando lustrare; idcirco praesenti opere, variarum historiarum amantes a peregrinandi labore, periculo, atque impensa liberavimus.

The would-be traveller may therefore welcome the opportunity to study foreign cities through the medium of fine illustrations which will make them more familiar to him than any number of words (acerrimo oculorum sensui, qui reliquos omnes, Aristotele teste, praestantia superat). In Braun's words, the work offers the student:

> accuratissimas urbium icones, quae in tabulis artificiose depictae, multo apertius de se praebent, quam si descriptione litteris tantum comprehensa, qualicumque et obscura earum cognitio quaereretur.

The visual image is accompanied by historical descriptions *historicae enarrationes*, to enable the reader to appreciate some of the major events in the city's past, as well as its situation and layout (praeter urbium oppidorumque situm, etiam ea, quae ad civitatem pertinent).

The student of politics, too, will benefit from a visual depiction, gaining insights into a city's history, building methods and defensive system (et historiarum augeatur cognitio, et quae optima aedificandi ratio sit, diversorum aedificiorum collatione, perspici queat).[2] To support his claim, Braun refers to Alexander the Great, who is said to have examined with utmost attention the places in which he was preparing to give battle and always wanted to have a map in front of him to help him draw up carefully judged plans (ut picturam illam comtemplando, ea dignosceret, quae cavenda, quaeve adeunda essent).

Portrayals of cities will also be of interest to merchants, helping them to discover how and where trade is carried on.

And no less important is the benefit to a city's own inhabitants. They will be able to acquire a deeper knowledge of the place in which they live, establish a better-informed relationship with their daily surroundings, and so feel more strongly rooted in their native soil (non peregrinus sed notus hospes).[3]

Right from the beginning the preface conveys the sense of a work which is to be enjoyed visually as well as to be read, and maybe the delight of the eye is the more important of the two. 'Spectatores lectoresque' are the audience to whom Braun commends the illustrations: outstanding topographical descriptions of famous cities (celebrium urbium oppidorumque topographicae descriptiones accuratissime delineatae).

There is a great sense of the city's value, reflected in the wording of the preamble regarding the city's origins and development as an institution: de primis urbium initiis, progressu et incremento.

> What makes the *Civitates* a watershed between medieval and modern culture are the reasons given for undertaking the work: first, that as an architectural achievement and product of man's creative genius the city is the highest expression of human society; secondly, that in conveying reality the visual image has a value of its own, surpassing any form of literary description.[4]

We could use Braun's own expressions of satisfaction to say how Simon Novellanus and Franz Hogenberg in their engravings have rendered their subjects with such wonderful artistry and vividness that we seem to be observing the cities themselves rather than images on a page.

> In quo quidnam ornamenti toti universo periti Architecti urbium, oppidorumque structura contulerint, artificiosae Simonis Novellani, et Francisci Hogenbergij manus, tam accurate ed ad vivum partium singularum proportione, et vicorum ordine ad amussim observato expresserunt, ut non icones et typi urbium sed urbes ipsae, admirabili coelaturae artificio, spectantium oculis subiectae appareant.[5].

Despite Braun's claim that some of their work is original (quas partim ipsi depinxerunt, partim ad ijs, sagaci diligentia conquisitas atque depictas acceperunt, qui singulas quasque urbes perlustrarunt), it has to be recognised that their work consists almost exclusively of reproductions of existing material of varying quality from different sources rather than drawings from life.

Although we cannot say for certain whether Hogenberg and Novellanus produced any original drawings (we have no evidence that they were landscape painters or topographers), it is quite evident that they worked largely from plans already published in other collections or in works on individual cities, or from original drawings supplied by scholars with a special interest in different cities.[6].

The techniques they employed are typical of the period, in keeping with the prevailing trend towards realistic portrayal of natural phenomena. In representing the city, they aim to reproduce its 'forms objectively, concretely depicting its component parts, although they adopt various solutions for conveying its inner structure'.[7]

In discussing the main criteria followed by the artists, Braun stresses how true to life their illustrations are, whether plans or views, stemming from precise observation of the city's surroundings, its site, walls, and the various public and private buildings:

> In quo topographicae urbium oppidorumque descriptiones, tam geometrica, quam perspectiva fingendi ratione, cum genuina situs, locorum, meonorium, publicorum et privatorum aedificiorum observatione, singulari artis industria atque praesidio sunt delineatae.[8]

In practice, the aim of accuracy is achieved to varying degrees, depending on the quality of the source materials, some not of the highest standard, on which, for reasons of overall economy, the engravers had to draw in forming the collection.

In number and in artistic effect, it is the perspective drawings which hold pride of place in the *Civitates*.

> Perspective to some extent fulfils man's age-old dream of being able to fly. It also responds to his conviction that it is beneficial to view his surroundings in their totality, from a commanding height or, better, from a vantage point in the sky. In these drawings, it is used to reveal the city from angles ranging between 30° and 60° above the horizontal. From this sort of exalted viewpoint we get a fairly clear impression of the urban layout (which forms a basic outline for the draughtsman), but what is most striking are the elevations of the buildings. When the drawing is executed with care and sufficient detail, we become aware of the city's underlying structural and aesthetic features, especially the volumes and combinations of forms which distinguish its individual parts.[9]

As noted earlier, the angle at which the observer views the subject varies from picture to picture, and the degree of elevation gives a more or less clear delineation of the city's ground plan.[10].

There are also many views drawn from a lower angle or even from ground level. These obviously give a much clearer impression of the sky line; the main civic and ecclesiatical buildings standing out from the general mass of dwelling houses.[11]

On the whole, each illustration is elegantly drawn, with a feel for its particular subject. The cities are shown in considerable detail, the blocks of buildings individually delineated and accurately located in relation to the street plan. The major buildings are generally recognisable by their architectural features.

In the case of cities viewed from higher vantage points, it is possible to make out the complexities of the city layout and the street system.

Great care has been taken in representing waterways, both natural and artificial, and the man-made structures, big and small, associated with them. Harbour works are vigorously depicted, usually enlivened by boats of different kinds.[12]

To complement the forms and extent of the city itself, the immediate surroundings are included in the picture, the features of the landscape clearly portrayed. The artist has not been confined by the city walls but has situated his subject in its natural environment, so heightening the realism of the scene and achieving a more lifelike effect.

Many of the engravings include small vignettes showing trades and occupations of different kinds or introduce human figures which lend animation to the scene. In the foreground of the larger illustrations, the artists have often depicted men and women wearing local dress.

In most cases the title is decorated with the arms of the city, usually drawn at the top of the page against a wide backdrop of open sky.

Scrolls, plaques and specula of different shapes and sizes, invariably enclosed in frames of exquisite design, contain brief descriptive or commendatory texts reiterating some of the main points of the *enarrationes* or reproducing references from classical literature, often touching on ancient history or the derivation of the city's name.[13]

The drawings of the cities themselves are furnished with a wealth of place names covering salient physical features, the main streets and squares, and buildings dedicated to religious or civic functions. This use of toponyms helps guide the reader in his analysis of the city, bringing to his notice the features worthy of attention and ascribing greater or lesser value to its different parts.

Sometimes the place names are listed in the margin, with numbered references to their location on the engraving itself.

At this point it is worth mentioning the language in which the place names are expressed. It is interesting that, whereas the whole body of written text is in Latin, the names of rivers, squares, streets and important buildings are often rendered in the vernacular.

This problem was very much in the minds of the publishers when the work was being prepared. In a letter dated 31 October 1571, Braun wrote to Ortelius for his authoritative opinion on whether it would be appropriate to use local languages (as he put it, to express 'propria locorum, templorum portarumque nomina idiomate [...] nativo').[14] His concern was more than just to avoid the difficulty of translating local names into Latin. He also had commercial considerations in mind: how the work would sell and what potential buyers would be requiring. He expected to find customers among the less cultured classes, who might be interested in buying individual engravings, as well as among men of learning.[15]

The finished work is a monument to the cities contained in it. Even allowing for the mixed quality of the source materials and the difficulties involved in drawing them into a harmonious whole, it is a masterpiece of the engraver's and publisher's skills. It was made available to the public in a black-and-white, printed edition, but some special copies were also coloured in by hand.

Hand-coloured copies obviously vary in quality, depending on the skill and experience of the artist. If the source drawings were not available for checking, there was also the risk of errors creeping in, especially in the colouring of heraldic features and costumes.[16]

When the work was done accurately by skilled artists the illustrations achieve a true pictorial quality: faithfully depicted in full colour, the cities seem even more to bear out the publishers' proud claim that they have been 'drawn from life'.

Let us now consider the form and content of the volume which opened the series, the volume which particularly concerns us here.

The richly decorated frontispiece consists of an elegant design of allegorical figures, with Architecture enthroned in their midst. The title stands out in capital letters. The *Civitates orbis terrarum* is obviously closely related, in more than name, to that other great work of geographical draughtsmanship, the *Theatrum orbis terrarum* by Abraham Ortelius, which had been published at Antwerp two years earlier.[17]

The work begins with Braun's preface (Georgius Bruin Agrippimensis benevolis lectoribus s.d.), an exposition of substance, from which we have already quoted a number of passages. This is followed by the dedication (Inperatori Caesari Rudulpho II P.F. Augusto [...] Georgius Braun et Franciscus Hohenbergius Dedic. consecrant.q.), a congratulatory poem in hexameters, written in dialogue form by Alexander Grapheus (Alexandri Grephei a secretis amplissimae Reipubl. Anverpianae in Orbis Terrarum Civitates Colloquium, Interloquutores Thaumastes, Panoptes), and the «tenor Privilegii».[18]

The introductory pages conclude with the printer's note: «Auctorum aere et impensis impressum, absolutumque est hoc opus Coloniae Agrippinae, Typis Theodori Graminaei, Calendis Augusti, Anno M.D.L.XXII».

Then begin the engravings, 58 in all, including plans and views of 139 cities, each accompanied by a descriptive text interspersed with historical information (the *enarrationes*).

The cities are presented in the order instituted by Ptolemy in his *Geography*, the arrangement subsequently adopted by Ortelius for his *Theatrum* and by other authors of atlases.[19]

First come the cities of Britain, followed by Portugal, Spain, France, the Netherlands, Germany, Eastern Europe and Italy, then Asia and Africa, and finally cities in recently discovered regions of the world. With few exceptions, this order is retained in the five sister volumes which continued to appear until the work was completed in 1618.[20] The volume published in 1572 differs in that it has no index, and the plates are not even numbered in sequence.

Although the cities illustrated are numerous, the work does not give the uniform coverage the title would seem to imply. It is true that the whole known world is included, but the different regions are not equally represented.

The work is inevitably Europe-centred. In fact, Western Europe is predominant, particularly Germany. Few Eastern European cities are included; even fewer from Asia and Africa; and there are only two from the New World. This is not just a matter of preference. We are bound to consider the general cultural context and the availability of source materials. The publishers themselves point out the relative originality of the undertaking, stating that the work shows the aspect of several cities, depictions of which few had ever set eyes on before.[21]

Where the better-known areas are concerned, the richness or poverty of the coverage cannot be ascribed only to the abundance or lack of source drawings. The choice of material was also greatly influenced by the content of existing publications.[22] It is fascinating to consider the relationship between the real world and the way in which it is represented, particularly the weight given to its different parts. The relationship is often conditioned by cultural perceptions which distort both size and importance.[23]

Braun himself shows an awareness of the mixed quality and incompleteness of the whole, and of his inevitable reliance on more or less suitable source materials, when he requests the collaboration of scholars in different countries. He asks them to send descriptions or pictures of their own cities, with the assurance that such material will be published in due course. He also states that some cities have been omitted, since it was not possible to obtain illustrative material on account of prevailing political or military conditions.[24]

The five subsequent volumes did much to fill out the roll of Cities covered and to some extent achieved a better balance between the different parts of the world.[25]

* * *

The magnificent series of engravings opens with a fine perspective drawing of London,[26] but this is the only British city represented in the first volume.

The Iberian Peninsula is represented by five plates covering 11 cities: Lisbon, Cascais and Belem, then Seville, Cadiz, Malaga, Toledo, Valladolid, Barcelona, Granada, Burgos and San Sebastian: a wide choice of cities depicted with vitality and sparkle, largely based on original works by Georg Hoefnagel.[27]

Turning to France, eight cities are featured: Paris and Lyon, with whole plates to themselves, and also Montpellier, Tours, Poitiers, Rouen, Nîmes and Bordeaux. The engravers have drawn on various sources, in particular the drawings of A. Du Pinet.[28]

An important place is given to the cities of Belgium (Brussels, Liège, Ghent, Bruges, Antwerp, Mons, Arras, Louvain and Malines) and Holland (Amsterdam and Utrecht illustrated with full-page engravings, together with 's-Hertogenbosch, Gorinchem, Brouwershaven and Groningen), many of which can be traced to the drawings contained in L. Guicciardini's *Descrittione*.[29]

Nevertheless, as we have already said, it is the German cities which form the largest group, more than 40 of them, giving a many-sided view of German city architecture, culled from a number of sources including Münster's *Cosmographia*.[30]

There is an interesting arrangement of no fewer than 13 Swiss cities, all brought together on a single plate.[31]

Austria is represented by views of Vienna and Salzburg,[32] Bohemia by Prague and Eger, Hungary by Buda.[33]

Italy is fairly well featured, with fine plates of many of its main cities and some ports.[34]

Closely linked with some of the Italian cities are views of Mediterranean and Near Eastern centres: after Malta, Rhodes and Famagusta come plates of Istambul and Jerusalem.[35]

The small but significant group of Asian cities includes Aden, Calicut, Cannanore, Diu, Goa and Hormuz, while Africa is represented by Anfao, Asilah, Azemmour, Cairo, Ceuta, Kilwa, Mina, Mombasa, Safi, Sala, Sofala and Tangier.[36]

The final plate shows two cities from the New World, Cuzco and Mexico City.[37]

As far as form is concerned, a certain unity of style distinguishes all the full-plate perspective drawings (London, Paris, Lyon, Brussels, Ghent, Bruges, Antwerp, Utrecht, Amsterdam, Magdeburg, Strasburg, Frankfurt-am-Main, Cologne, Augsburg, Milan, Venice, Rome, Ancona, Naples, Istambul, Messina and Cairo). These are all viewed from an elevated vantage point, so that we can clearly discern the street network and overall layout of the city as well as the features of the buildings.[38] Most of the other illustrations are drawn from a lower angle though still high enough to embrace the entire city and consist of views or prospects tending to emphasise the silhouette of the rooflines against the sky. In freshness of composition, delicacy of draughtsmanship, quality of expression and realism, they are in no way inferior to the larger illustrations.

This was the first time so ambitious a work had been attempted. The result is a full and varied treatment of the subject, despite its lack of proportion and biassed viewpoint.

With the publication of the *Civitates*, representations of the city came to have a definite place alongside the great geographical maps of the period. The effects can be seen in subsequent map publishing and in some of the great wall-painting cycles of the 16th century.[39]

Quite apart from its major contributions to the history of the visual image, the *Civitates* has played a fundamental and quite unique role in our understanding of cities and their history.

Lelio Pagani

NOTES

1) *Civitates orbis terrarum*, Cologne, 1572, from G. Braun's preface.

2) According to Braun, there could be great benefits in the struggle to defend Christian cities from the depredations of the Turk ('earum urbium, quae a truculentissimis nationibus, Christianis sunt ereptae').

3) L. Nuti, 'Alle origini del Grand Tour: immagini e cultura della città italiana negli atlanti e nelle cosmografie del secolo XVI', *Storia Urbana*, 27, 1984, p. 16.

4) *Ibid.*, p. 17.

5) From the preface to the *Civitates*.

6) L. Nuti, *op. cit.*, p. 19.

7) L. Gambi, 'L'immagine della città', *Cenobio*, XXIV (4), Oct.-Dec. 1985, pp. 297-8.

8) From the preface to the *Civitates*.

9) L. Gambi, *op. cit.*, p. 305.

10) R.V. Tooley, Preface, in Braun-Hogenberg, *Civitates orbis terrarum, the towns of the world, 1572-1618*, with an introduction by R.A. Skelton, Cleveland, New York, 1966, p. V.

11) Some views, especially in later volumes, could fairly be described as landscape compositions, for instance the scenes drawn by G. Hoefnagel. See A. Popham, 'Georg Hoefnagel and the *Civitates orbis terrarum*', *Maso Finiguerra* I (2-3), 1936, p. 199.

12) R.V. Tooley, *op. cit.*, p. V.

13) Most of the full-page engravings have several insets of this kind. The descriptions tend to be stereotypes drawn from earlier depictions of particular cities.

14) See A. Popham, *op. cit.*, p. 185.

15) 'Ita siquidem futuru ut queam doctis, tam rudioribus una satisfiat. Illis quidem, quia in dorso descriptiones habebant latinas, his vero, quia suam quisque patriam, artificiose delineatam, cum notis sibi locorum significationibus, videbit. Huius autem instituti utilitatem, tum percipi posse existimo, ubi separatim civitatum picturae vendutur, quae non ita gratae civibus erant, si nihil eorum quae legunt, intelligat'. From Braun's letter to Ortelius referred to in the text.

16) R.V. Tooley, *op. cit.*, p.V. The writer points out that the colours may have been applied at the time of publication or later. The colouring is generally vivid, though some areas are left white. In some cases, the finer points of the engraving have been obscured as a result of colouring. To quote Tooley, 'nevertheless special copies were prepared for important personages, and in assessing the value of a particular copy quality makes a great difference, whether plain or coloured'.

17) See A. Popham, *op. cit.*, and J. H. Hessels, 'Abrahami Ortelii geographi antverpensis et virorum eruditorum.... epistulae', *Ecclesiae Londino - Batavae Archivum*, I, Cambridge, 1887.

18) 'Ne quisquam [..] librum totius universi urbium et oppidorum picturas continentur hoc titulo, Civitates Orbis Terrarum, Coloniae Anno Domini 1572, impressum auctoribus Francisco Hogenbergo, Simone Novellano et Georgio Bruin vel coniunctim vel divisim, civitatum etiam historicas enarrationes quocumque idiomate, decim annis...'.

19) See Braun's letter to Ortelius, dated 6 February 1572, quoted by J.H. Hessels in the work referred to above. Also R.A. Skelton's introduction to Braun-Hogenberg, *Civitates...*, p.X.

20) *Ibid.* It is also interesting to note the arrangement of the cities in the region-by-region index printed at the end of the VIth volume of the *Civitates*, which came out in 1618 (*Theatri praecipuarum totius mundi liber sextus*).

21) Preface to the *Civitates*.

22) In the case of Italy, great deference was paid to works such as L. Alberti's *Descrittione di tutta Italia, nella quale si contiene il sito di essa, l'origine, e le Signorie della Città ed delle Castella*, published at Bologna in 1550.

23) L. Nuti, *op. cit.*, p. 10.

24) Preface to the *Civitates*.

25) See R.A. Skelton, *op. cit.*, Appendix B, 'Classified List of Plans and Views', pp. XXVIII-XLIII. This contains an index of the plates arranged according to the countries to which the various cities belong. The index at the end of the VIth volume of the *Civitates* in also worth studying from this point of view.

26) J.P. Marks, *The map of mid-sixteenth century London*, London Topographical Society, 1964.

27) According to R.A. Skelton, *op. cit.*, pp. XXIX-XXX, we can ascribe to Hoefnagel the source drawings for the engravings of Burgos, Granada, San Sebastian, Toledo and probably Barcelona.

28) There is evidence that the depictions of Bordeaux, Montpellier, Poitiers and Tours are drawn from originals by Du Pinet (A. Du Pinet, *Plantz, pourtraitz et descriptions de plusieurs villes et forteresses*, Lyon, 1564); Lyon appears to be based on an engraving by B.v.d. Bosch, 1550; Nìmes and Paris on Münster's *Cosmographia*, published in 1569; Rouen is probably drawn from a work by G. Hoefnagel (see R.A. Skelton, *op. cit*, p. XXXI).

29) Antwerp, Bruges, Brussels, Ghent, Louvain, Amsterdam and 's-Hertogenbosch can be traced to plans reproduced in L. Guicciardini's *Descrittione di tutti i Paesi Bassi*, 1567; Malines is probably drawn from an original by Hoefnagel and Utrecht from an engraving by M. van Hoorn, 1569 (see R.A. Skelton, *op. cit.*, p. XXXII). Liège is based on an engraving sent to Braun by Gerard von Groesbeck, as evidenced in the accompanying description.

30) See S. Münster's *Cosmographia*, published at Basel in 1550. This work was the source for the depictions of Koblenz, Erfurt, Frankfurt an der Oder, Fulda, Heidelberg, Lindau, Lüneberg, Marburg, Nordlingen, Speyer, Trier, Worms and Würzburg. The others are drawn for the most part from maps by artists such as Hans Rogel, Peter Sitzer, and Hans and Martin Weigel. (R.A. Skelton, *op. cit.*, pp. XXXIV-XXXVII).

31) The *Schwzer Chronik* by Johann Stumpf, 1548, will repay attention.

32) The view of Vienna had already appeared in Münster's *Cosmographia*, published in 1550, based on a 1547 work by A. Hirsvogel; The view of Salzburg is based on an engraving by M. Secznagel, previously published as plate 28 in the 1570 edition of Ortelius' *Theatrum* (R.A. Skelton, *op. cit.*, p. XXXVII). On the plate with views of Munich, Freising etc., you will notice an empty space, probably reserved for the city of Innsbruck. A section of the *enarrationes* relating to this plate is in fact dedicated to 'Oenipons/Inspruk'.

33) The illustration of Prague is drawn from an original by J. Caper and M. Petrle (1562); that of Buda is based on the work of E. Schön (R.A. Skelton, p. XXXVIII).

34) L. Nuti, *op. cit.*, p. 21, gives an analysis of the Italian cities illustrated in the *Civitates*. For more detail, it is worth referring to material on individual cities in the volumes of the series 'Le città nella storia d'Italia', edited by C. De Seta and published by Laterza. Among others, these refer to source works by J. Fontana for Ancona, S. Arquer for Cagliari, G.F. Camocio for Rome, G. Argaria for Messina, A. Lafreri for Milan and Naples, B. Zaltieri for Venice, and B. Bonhomme for Parma. See also R.V. Tooley, 'Maps in Italian atlases of the sixteenth century', *Imago Mundi*, III, 1939, pp. 12-47.

35) For the source materials in this case we must look to Venetian authors, such as Vavassore, Camocio and Zenoi, who produced single maps and compendia known as 'isolari'. The illustration of Constantinople derives, via Münster, from an original work by G.A. Vavassori (1520). The depiction of Jerusalem, which juxtaposes the ancient and modern cities, is based on an engraving by P. Laicksteen and G. Grooten (1570) (R.A. Skelton, *op. cit.*, p. XVLII).

36) In his preface, Braun expresses gratitude to Costantin von Lyschirchen for supplying the views of the Asian and African cities. (For his sources, see Skelton, pp. XLII-XLIII). For Cairo, Braun could draw on *La vera descriptione dela gran Cita del Caiero* drawn by D. della Greche in 1548 and printed by Matteo Pagan at Venice in 1549. Also of interest is L. Micara's 'Il Cairo nella *Chorographia* di Pellegrino Brocardi (1556)', *Storia della città*, 46, April-June 1988, pp. 7-18.

37) Mexico City had already been illustrated in B. Bordon's *Libro nel qual si ragiona di tutte le isole del mondo*, Venice, 1528. Likewise, a plan of Cuzco had appeared in volume III of G.B. Ramusio's *Navigationi et Viaggi*, Venice, 1556.

38) The only exception is Liège which, though occupying a full page, is in fact viewed in perspective from ground level.

39) R. Almagià discusses the relationship between the work of E. Danti and the *Civitates*, with particular reference to an important cycle of paintings by the artist, in *Le pitture murali della Galleria delle Carte geografiche; Monumenta Cartografica Vaticana*, III, Vatican City, 1952.

BIBLIOGRAPHY

— R. Almagià, *Carte geografiche a stampa di particolare pregio o rarità dei secoli XVI e XVII esistenti nella Biblioteca Apostolica Vaticana, Monumenta Cartographica Vaticana*, II, Vatican City, 1948.

— R. Almagià, *Concetto e indirizzi della Geografia attraverso i tempi* (1947) in *Scritti geografici*, Roma, 1961, pp. 553-582.

— R. Almagià, *Le pitture murali della Galleria delle carte geografiche, Monumenta Cartographica Vaticana*, III, Vatican City, 1952.

— *Atlas des villes de la Belgique au XVI siècle*, ed. C. Ruelens, Brussels, 1884-1924.

— F. Bachmann, *Die Alten Städtebilder*, Leipzig, 1939 (reprinted Stuttgart, 1965).

— L. Bagrow, *History of Cartography* rev. and enlarged by R.A. Skelton, London, 1964.

— O. Baldacci, *Introduction to an exhibition of antique atlases, in XX Congr. Geogr. It., Rome, 29 March - 30 April 1967: Exhibition on Ptolemy and antique atlases*, Rome, 1967, pp. 41-87.

— R.Z. Becker, *Holzschnitte alter deutscher Meister in den Original-Platten gesammelt von Hans Albrecht von Derschau*, Gotha, 1808-16.

— G.L. Burkel, *The Making of the Dutch Towns*, London, 1956.

— E. Borea, *Stampa figurativa e pubblico dalle origini all'affermazione del Cinquecento*, in *Storia dell'arte italiana*, II, *L'artista e il pubblico*, Turin, 1979, pp. 319-413.

— C. Buttafava, *Visioni di città nelle opere d'arte del Medioevo e del Rinascimento*, Milan, 1963.

— M. Casciato, *La cartografia olandese tra Cinquecento e Seicento*, «Storia della città», n. 12-13, 1979, pp. 5-18.

— T. Coletta, *Atlanti di Città del Cinquecento*, Naples, 1984.

— F. De Dainville, *Le langage des géographes, Termes, signes, couleurs des cartes anciennes, 1500-1800*, Paris, 1964.

— J. Denuce, *Oud-Nederlandsche Kaartmakers met betrekking to Plantijn*, Antwerpen-'s-Gravenhage, 1912-13 (reprinted Amsterdam, 1964).

— C. De Seta, *Significati e simboli della rappresentazione topografica negli Atlanti dal XVI al XVII secolo*, in *Città capitali*, edited by the author, Rome-Bari, 1985, pp. 17-54.

— *Deutschland vor drei Jahrhunderten. Seine Städte, Flüsse und Wälder betrachten von Willem und Joan Blaeu, Georg Braun, Franz Hogenberg und Joris Hoefnagel*, Berlin, 1971.

— F. Ehrle, *Roma prima di Sisto V: la pianta di Roma Du Perac-Lafréry del 1577*, in *Collectanea variae doctrinae Leoni S. Olschki bibliopolae florentino sexagenario*, Munich, 1921.

— G. Ferro, I. Caraci, *Ai confini dell'orizzonte, Storia delle esplorazioni e della geografia*, Milan, 1979.

— E. Fétis, *Les artistes belges à l'étranger: Georges Hoefnagel*, «Bulletin de l'Académie Royale des Sciences, des Lettres et des Beaux-Arts de Belgique», XXI, 1854, pp. 978-1012.

— R. Fruin, *Nederlandsche steden in de XVIe eeuw: plattegronden van Jacob van Deventer*, Facsimile edition, 's Gravenhage, 1916-23.

— L. Gallois, *Les géographes allemandes de la Renaissance*, Paris, 1890 (reprinted, Amsterdam, 1961).

— L. Gambi, *La città da immagine simbolica a proiezione urbanistica*, in *Storia d'Italia*, VI, *Atlante*, Turin, 1976, pp. 217-28.

— L. Gambi, *L'immagine della città*, «Cenobio», XXXIV, 4, Oct./Dec. 1985, pp. 284-314.

— E. Guidoni, A. Marino, *Storia dell'urbanistica, Il Cinquecento*, Rome-Bari, 1982.

— E. Guidoni, A. Marino, *Storia dell'urbanistica, Il Seicento*, Rome-Bari, 1979.

— B. van't Hoff, *Bijdrage tot de dateering van de oudere Nederlandsche stadsplattegronden*, Nederlandsch Archievenblad, XLIX, 1941-42, pp. 29-68, 97-150.

— B. van't Hoff, *Jacob van Deventer, Keizerlijk-Koninklijk geograaf* 's - Gravenhage, 1953.

— J. Keuning, *The «Civitates» of Braun and Hogenberg*, «Imago Mundi», XVII, 1963, pp. 41-44.

— J. Keuning, *XVI Century Cartography in the Netherlands*, «Imago Mundi», IX, 1952.

— O. Klose - L. Martius, *Ortansichten und Stadtpläne der Herzogtümer Schleswig, Holstein und Lauenburg*, Neumünster, 1962.

— C. Koeman, *Collections of Maps and Atlases in the Netherlands, their History and Present State*, Leiden, 1961.

— C. Koeman, *The History of Abraham Ortelius and his «Theatrum Orbis Terrarum»*, Lausanne, 1964 (Introduction to a facsimile edition).

— H. Lempertz, *Das Städtebuch von Georg Braun und Franz Hogenberg und die darin enthaltene Abbildung und Beschreibung Werdens*, «Annalen des Historischen Vereins für den Niederrhein», XXXVI, 1881, pp. 179-86.

— L. Nuti, *Alle origini del Grand Tour: immagini e cultura della città italiana negli atlanti e nelle cosmografie del secolo XVI*, «Storia Urbana», 27, 1984, pp. 3-33.

— J.A. Pinto, *Origin and Development of the Iconographic City Plan*, «Journal of the Society of Architectural Historians», XXXV, 1976, pp. 35-50.

— A. Popham, *Georg Hoefnagel and the Civitates Orbis Terrarum*, «Maso Finiguerra», I, 1936, 2-3, pp. 183-201.

— M. Quaini, *L'Italia dei cartografi*, in *Storia d'Italia*, VI, *Atlante*, Turin, 1976, pp. 5-50.

— P. Revelli, *La geografia del Cinquecento*, «Boll. Soc. Geogr. It.», 1913, pp. 98-124 and 231-265.

— G. Ricci, *Cataloghi di città, stereotipi etnici e gerarchie urbane nell'Italia di antico regime*, «Storia urbana», 18, 1982, pp. 3-33.

— G. Strauss, *Sixteenth-Century Germany: its topography and topographers*, Madison, 1959.

— R.V. Tooley, *Maps and Map-makers*, London, 1949 (7th ed. 1982).

— R.V. Tooley, *Maps in Italian Atlases of the Sixteenth Century*, «Imago Mundi», III, 1939, pp. 12-47.

— C. Wauwermans, *Histoire de l'école cartographique belge et anversoise du XVI siècle*, (1895) reprinted Amsterdam, 1974.

— E. Wiepen, *Bartholomäus Bruyn der Ältere und Georg Braun*, «Jahrbuch des Kölnischen Geschichtsvereins», III, 1916, pp. 95-153.

*   *   *

— A. Bartsch, *Le peintre graveur*, Vienna, 1803-21 (reprinted Hildesheim, 1970).

— P. Bellini, *Stampatori e mercanti di stampe in Italia nei secoli XVI e XVII*, «I quaderni del conoscitore di stampe», 26, 1975, pp. 19-45.

— E. Benezit, *Dictionnaire critique et documentaire des peintres, sculpteurs et graveurs*, Paris, 1911-55.

— P. Colin, *La gravure et les graveurs*, Brussels, 1916-18.

— A. J. J. Delen, *Histoire de la gravure dans les anciens Pays-Bas et dans les provinces Belges des origines jusqu'à la fin du XVI siècle*, Paris-Brussels, 1924-34 (reprinted, Paris, 1969).

— J. G. T. Graesse, *Trésor de livres rares et précieux*, Berlin, 1922 (reprinted Milan, 1950).

— A. M. Hind, *An Introduction to a History of Woodcut*, London, 1935.

— A. M. Hind, *Early Italian Engravings*, London, 1938-48 (reprinted, 1970).

— A. M. Hind, *Engraving in England in the 16th and 17th Centuries*, Part. I, Cambridge, 1952.

— F. W. Hollstein, *Dutch and Flemish Etchings, Engravings and Woodcuts, 1450-1700*, Amsterdam, 1949.

— F.W. Hollstein, *German Etchings, Engravings and Woodcuts, 1450-1700*, Amsterdam, 1954.

— G. Milesi, *Dizionario degli incisori*, Bergamo, 1982.

— A. Petrucci, *Panorama dell'incisione italiana, Il Cinquecento*, Rome, 1964.

— S. Samek Ludovici, *Arte del libri, Tre secoli di storia del libro illustrato dal Quattrocento al Seicento*, Milan, 1974.

— U. Thieme - F. Becker, *Allgemeines Lexikon der Bildenden Künstler*, Leipzig, 1907-50.

*   *   *

— Braun and Hogenberg, *Civitates Orbis Terrarum, The Towns of the World, 1572-1618*, with an Introduction by R.A. Skelton, Cleveland - New York, 1966.

— Bruin, Van Der Neuwel, Hogenberg, *Civitates Orbis Terrarum*. Full facsimile edition of original in the Biblioteca Civica, Bergamo, edited by L. Chiodi, Bergamo, 1977.

— Georg Braun and Franz Hogenberg, *Beschreibung und contrafactur der vornembster Stät der Welt*, introduction by M. Schefold, Plochingen, 1965-70.

— *Alte Europäische Städtebilder. 24 farbige Blätter nach Georg Braun und Franz Hogenberg*, ed. R. Oehme, Haarlem, 1954.

— *Old European Cities*, Twenty four 16th Century city maps and texts from the «Civitates Orbis Terrarum» of G. Braun and F. Hogenberg, with an interpretation by A. Hibbert and a description by R. Oehme of early map-making techniques, London, 1955 (reprinted 1965).

— *Old European Cities*, Thirty two 16th Century city maps and texts from the *Civitates Orbis Terrarum* (...) with a description by R. Oehme of early map-making techniques, London, 1965.

* This volume contains 29 of the 58 plates from G. Braun and F. Hogenberg's *Civitates Orbis Terrarum*, published by Th. Gramineus of Cologne in 1572. For the sake of completeness, a list of the remaining plates, reproduced in the same way in a separate volume entitled *Civitates Orbis Terrarum, Cities of the World; Europe and America*, is given below.

The plates are reproduced from an original preserved in the Biblioteca Civica A. Mai at Bergamo, accession number Cinq. 7. 761. The hand colouring of this copy is particularly fine and clear.

A full facsimile edition of this magnificent work, with an introduction by Luigi Chiodi, was made in 1977.

We would like to express our sincere thanks to the Director of the Biblioteca Civica, Bergamo, for allowing us to reproduce the plates and so make them more widely known.

TABVLAE

POS
TERI
TATI

CON
SVL
TV

ORNAMENT. ORB. TERR.

CIVITA
TES OR
BIS TER
RARVM

ARCIVM INVENTRIX.

OPIDOR. AVCTOR.

CONSOCIAT. HVMANI GEN. ORIGO.

ARCHITECT. RVDIM.

DOMICIL. TYROCIN.

LVTETIA, vulgari nomine Paris, vrbs Galliæ maxima, Sequanâ nauigabili flumine irrigatur, nobili gente, mercatorû frequêtia vniuersitate excellenti, stupendi operis templo B. Mariæ, Palatio Regio, alijs que præstantißimis ædificijs, tribunali æquißimorum Judicum, & pulcherrimis epitaphijs, florentißima

PARIS pour vraÿ est la maisõ royalle,   Inde en estude, & en poetes Romme,   Fecunde en vin, doulce en ses Citoÿens
Du dieu Phœbus en splendeur radiale   Athenes lors en mait tres sçauãt homme,   Fertile en bled, & en maintz daultres
Cest Gÿrrhea pleine de bons espritz,   Rozier mondain, baulme du firmament,   biens.
Tressigoureux, faisans diuers escriptz,   Vniuersel, de Sidon lornement
Cest Chrysea en metaulx habondante   Tres habondante en viures et breuuaiges,   Cum Priuilegio
Grece de pris en liures florissant   Riche en beaulx champs & fluuieux riuages

I

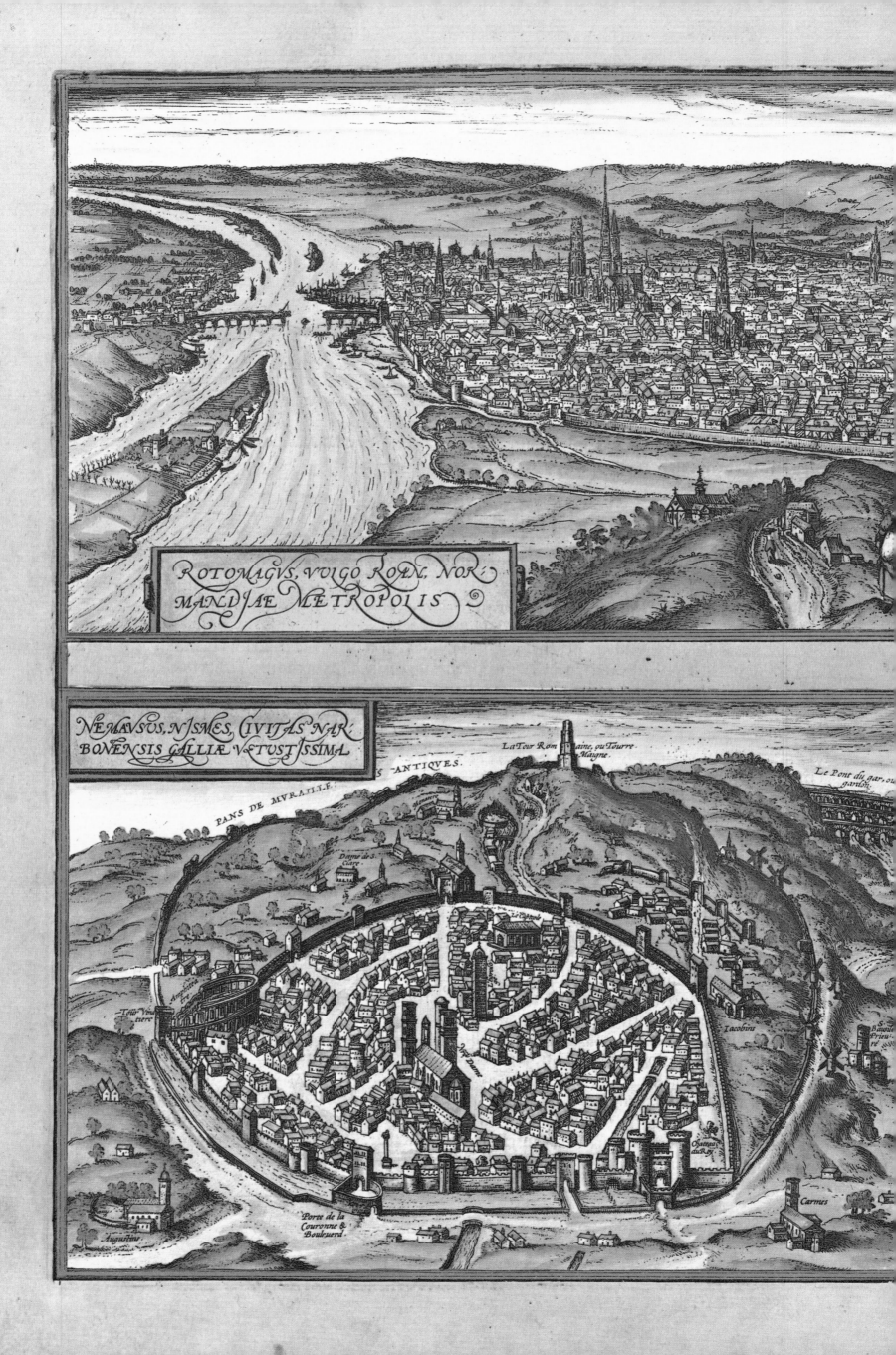

ROTOMAGVS, VVLGO ROAN, NOR-
MANDIAE METROPOLIS

NEMAVSVS, NISMES, CIVITAS NAR-
BONENSIS GALLIÆ VETVSTISSIMA

PANS DE MVRAILLE

S ANTIQVES

La Tour Romaine, ou Tourre
Maigne.

Le Pont du gar, ou
gardon.

Dame de S.
Clare.

Le Capitole

Toir Vinai-
tiere

Iacobins

S. Bauile
Prieure-
re

Chateau
duct

Carmes

Porte de la
Couronne &
Boulvard.

Augustins.

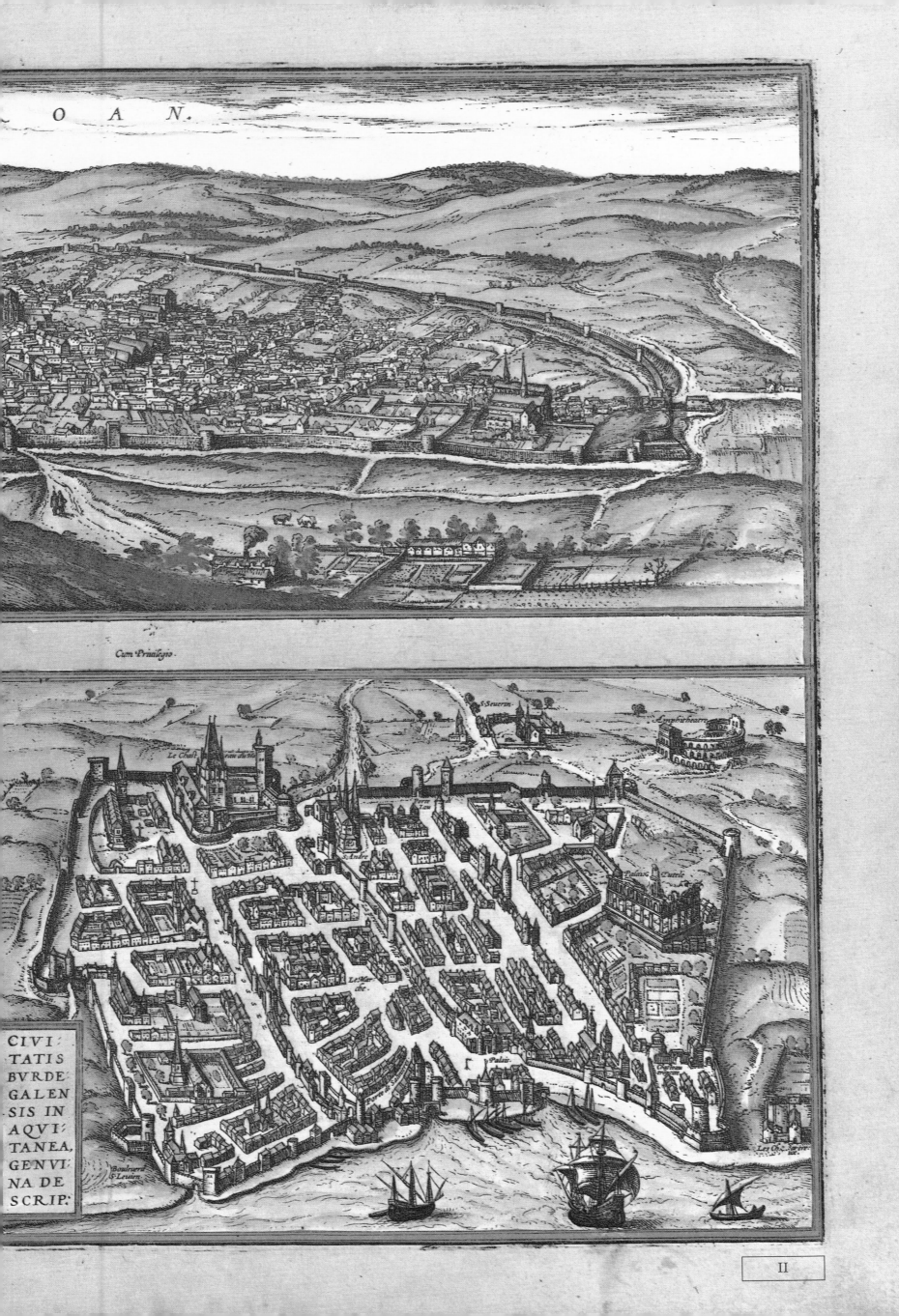

OAN.

Cum Priuilegio.

CIVI:
TATIS
BVRDE:
GALEN:
SIS IN
AQVI:
TANEA,
GENVI:
NA DE:
SCRIP:

II

ARGENTORATVM.

ARGENTORATVM, cuius
ob antiquitatem Ptolemeus, D Hie-
ronymus, Orosius, Eutropius, Mar-
cellinus, et alij meminêre, Alsatiæ
Metropolis, apud præterfluentem
Rhenum, alijs, Argentina, aut,
si quis ex re, nomen commutare
velit, Laurentina, sed vulgo
Strasburgum dicta; vrbs virtute,
maiis fratuum prudentia, ac inte-
gritate, honestis studijs, ac nobili scho-
la inclyta.

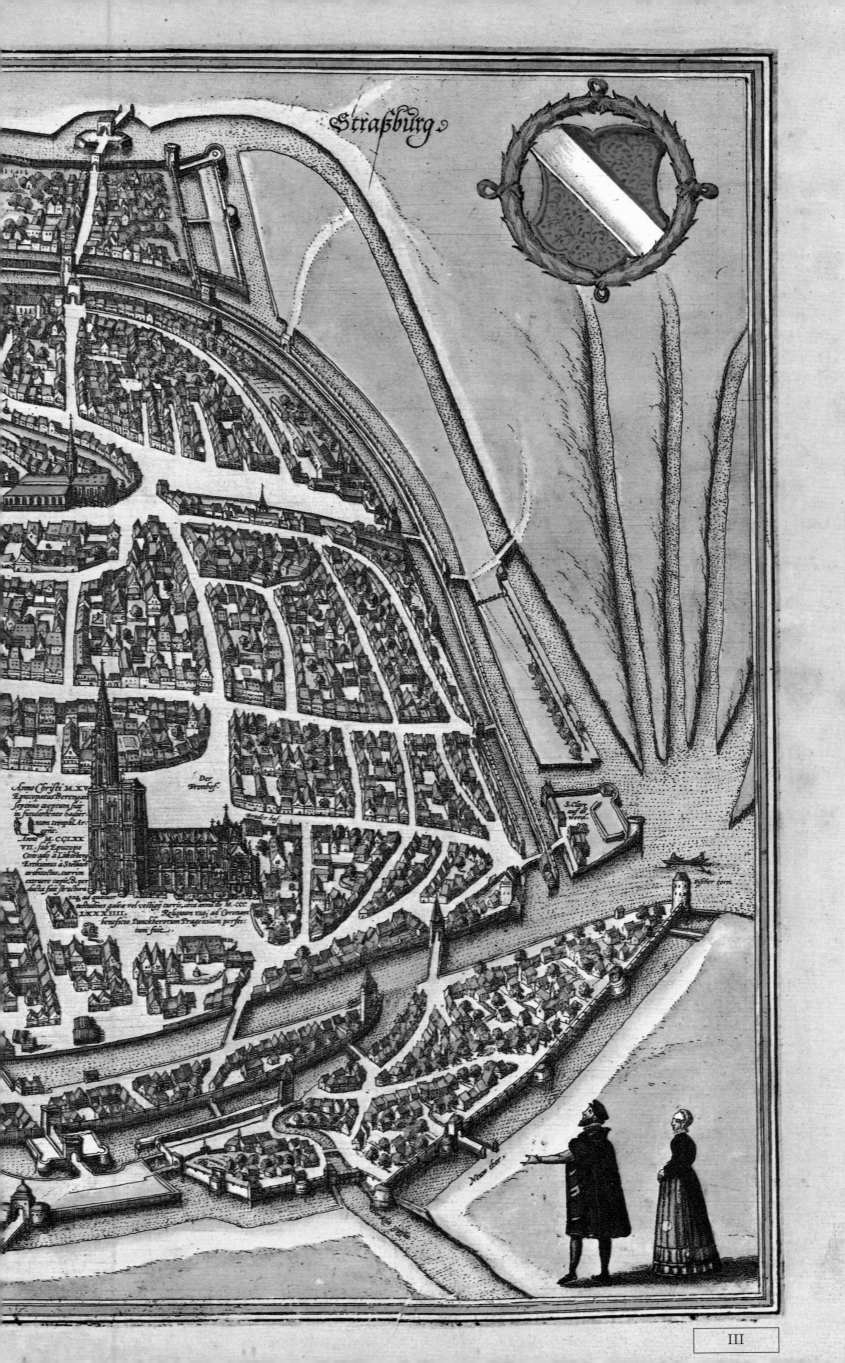

Straßburg

Anno Christi M.XV
Epicopatus Berengar-
servatus augens, fe-
in fundamento bast
Novum templi Ar-
gen-
Anno M.CCLXX
VII. sub Epicopo
Conrado à Liebfen-
Artificum è Stein-
architectus, turris
cum suo interiori
Ritu fait structura

turris, ad quem
turlatus galea vel cœlestis turris, circa annis M.CCC
LXXXIIII. Reliquum vero, ad Coronam
benefico Puncktherium Pragensium, perfec-
tum fuit.

Der
Grünhof.

Bruder hof.

S. Clar
auf d'Werd

Fischer torn.

Newe Seel.

III

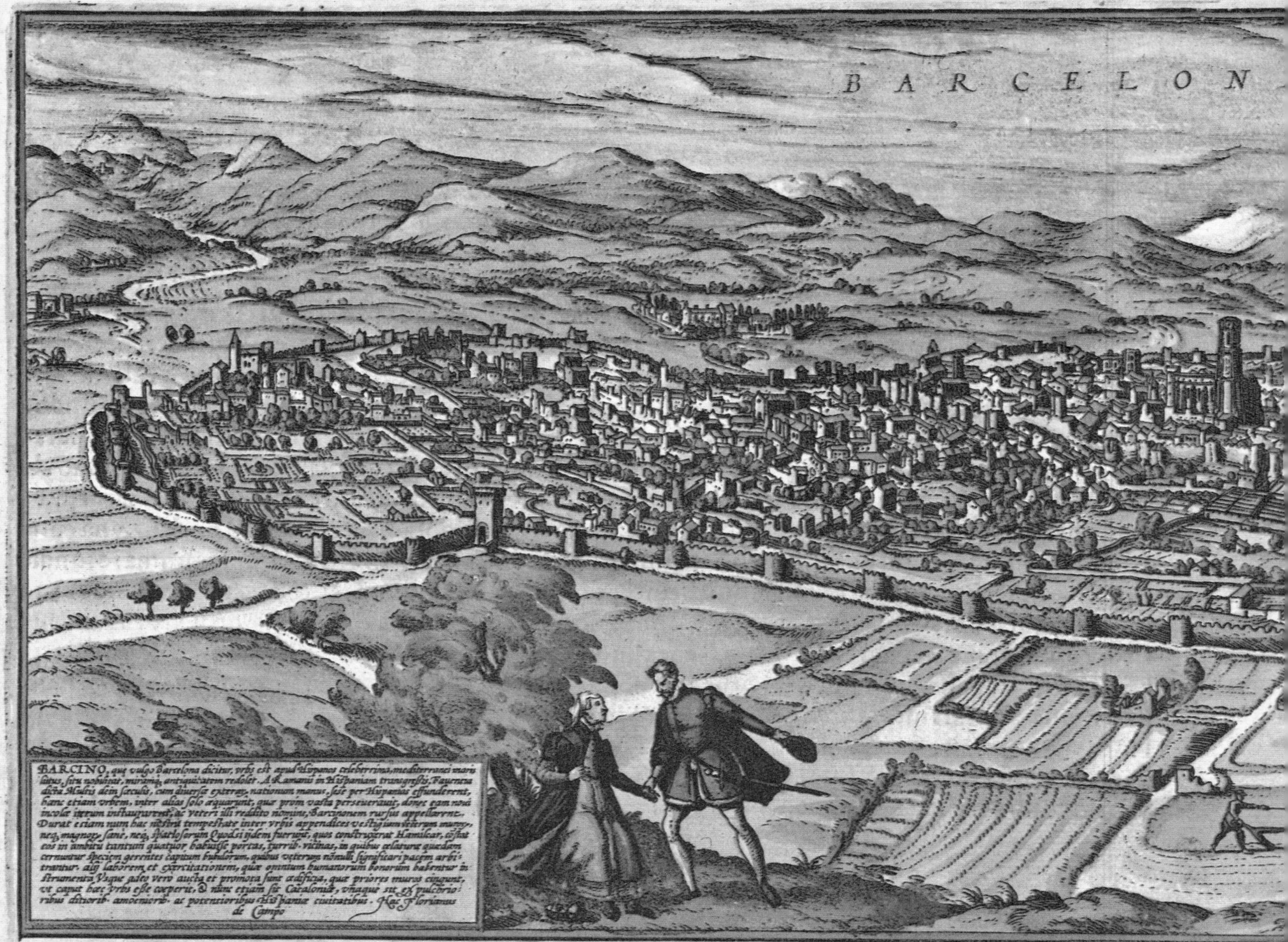
B A R C E L O N
BARCINO, quę vulgo Barcelona dicitur, vrbs est apud Hispanos celeberrima, mediterranei maris
littus, situ nobilitat, miramq; antiquitatem redolet. A Romanis in Hispaniam transgressis, Fauentia
dicta. Multis dein seculis, cum diuersę exterarq; nationum manus, sese per Hispanias effunderent,
hanc etiam vrbem, inter alias solo æquarunt, quæ prius vasta perseuerauit, donec eam noui
incolæ iterum instaurarent, ac veteri illi reddito nomine, Barcinonem rursus appellarent.
Durat etiam num hac nostra tempestate inter vrbis appendices vestigium veterum murorum,
neq; magnorum sane, neq; spatiosorum. Quod si iidem fuerunt, quos construxerat Hamilcar, constat
eos in ambitu tantum quatuor habuisse portas, turrib. vicinas, in quibus cælaturæ quædam
cernuntur speciem gerentes capitum bubulorum, quibus veterum nonnulli significari pacem arbi-
trantur. alij laborem et exercitationem, quæ omnium humanorum bonorum habentur in-
strumenta. Vsque adeo vero aucta et promota sunt ædificia, quæ priores muros cingunt,
vt caput hæc vrbs esse cœperit, & nunc etiam sit Cataloniæ, vnaque sit ex pulcrio-
ribus ditiorib. amoenioribq. ac potentioribus Hispaniæ ciuitatibus. Hæc Florianus
de Campo

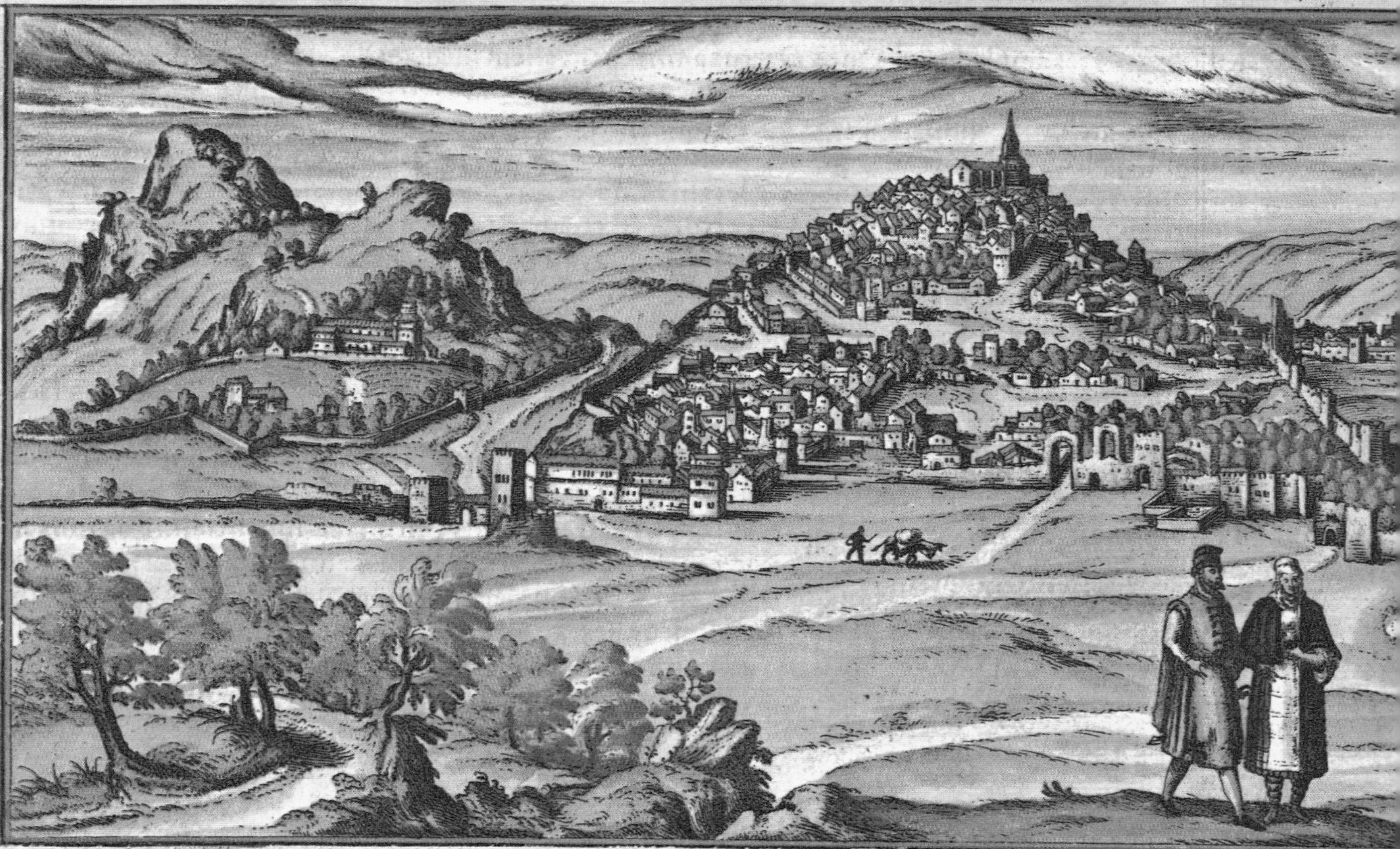

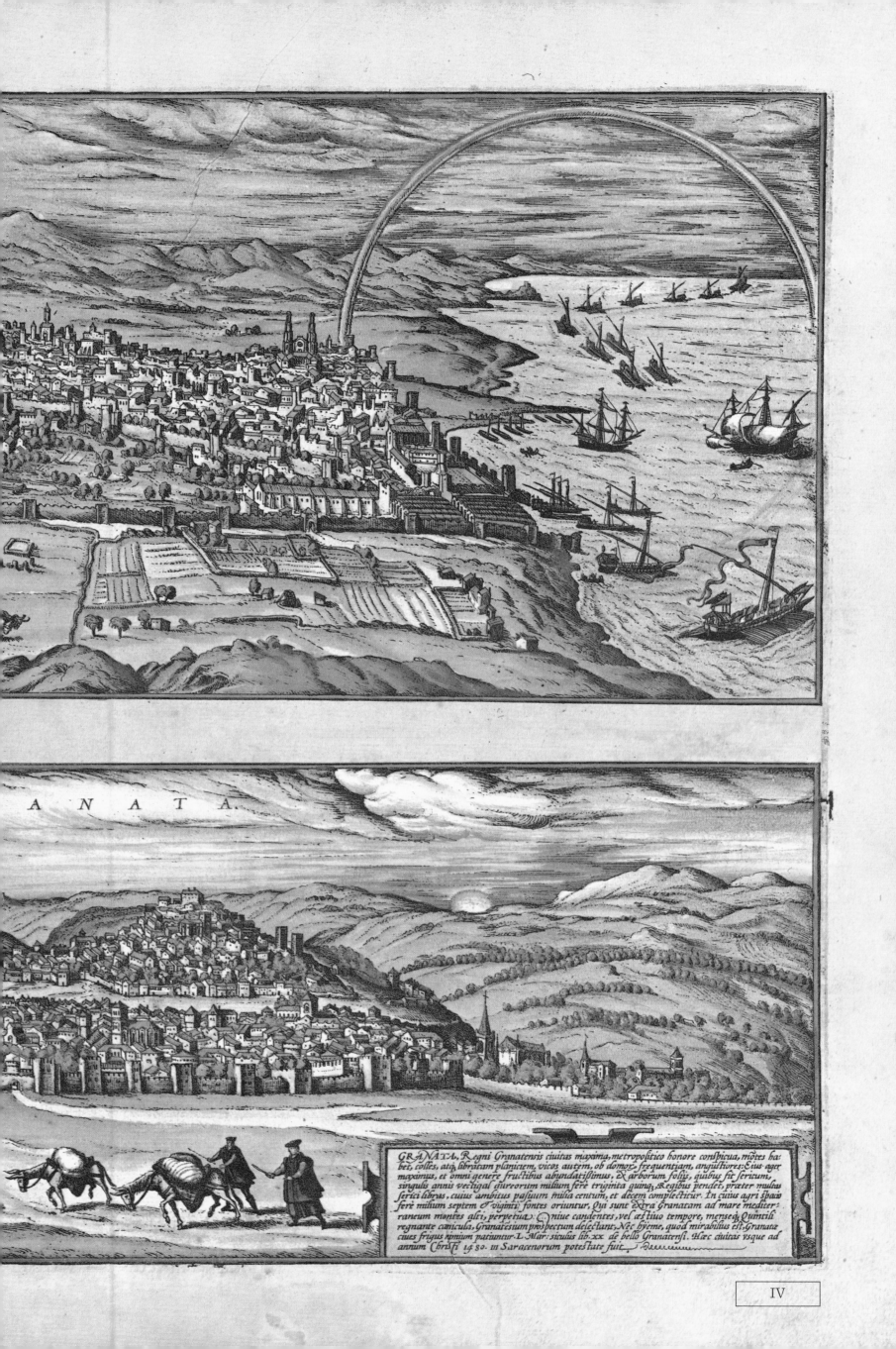

ANATA.

GRANATA, Regni Granatensis ciuitas maxima, metropolitico honore conspicua, mōtes habet, colles, atq́ libratam planiciem, vicos autem, ob domoṛ frequentiam, angustiores. Eius ager
maximus, et omni genere fructibus abundatiſsimus. & arborum folijs, quibus fit sericum,
singulis annis vectigal aureorum milium fere triginta quinq́. Regibus pendet, praeter multas
serici libras, cuius ambitus paſsuum milia centum, et decem complectitur. In cuius agri ſpacio
fere milium septem & viginti fontes oriuntur, Qui sunt extra Granatam ad mare mediter-
raneum montes alti, perpetua q́ niue candentes, vel aestiuo tempore, menseq́ Quintili
regnante canicula, Granatēsium prospectum delectant, Nec hyeme, quod mirabilius est, Granatæ
ciues frigus nimium patiuntur. L. Mar: siculus lib. xx. de bello Granatensi. Hæc ciuitas vsque ad
annum Christi 1480. in Saracenorum potestate fuit.

IV

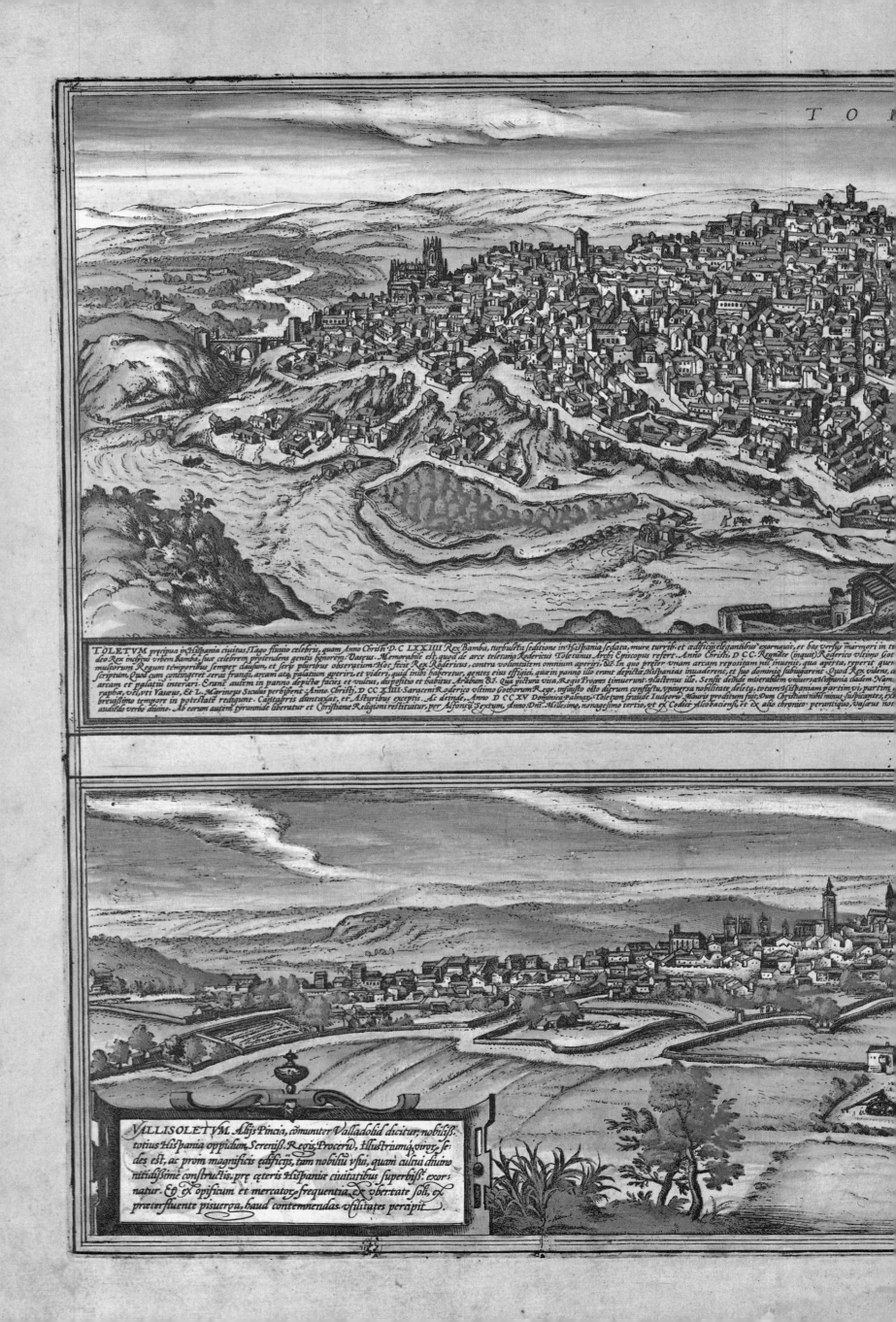

TOLETVM præcipua in Hispania ciuitas, Tago fluuio celebris, quam Anno Christi D.C LXXIIII Rex Bamba, turbulenta seditione in Hispania sedata, muro, turrib. et ædificijs elegantibus exornauit, et hos versus marmori in tu...
deo Rex incisus orbem Bamba, suæ celebrem protendens gentis honorem. Vascus. Memorabile est, quod de arce teletania Rodericus Toletanus Archi Episcopus refert. Anno Christi, D CC. Regnâte (inquit) Roderico vltimo Got...
multorum Regum temporibus semper clausum, et serijs pluribus obseratum. Hoc fecit Rex Rodericus, contra voluntatem omnium aperiri. Q? In quo præter vnam arcam repositam nil inuenit, qua aperta, reperit quer...
scriptum, Quod cum contingeret seras frangi, arcam atq; palatium aperiri, et videri, quid inibi haberetur, gentes eius effigiei, quæ in panno illo erant depictæ Hispanias inuaderent, et suo dominio subiugarent. Quod Rex videns, a...
arcam et galatiu interari. Erant autem in panno depictæ facies et vultus, dispositio et habitus Arabum &? Qua pictura visa, Regis Proceres timuerunt. Hactenus ille. Sensit deinde miserablem vniuersaHispania cladem. Nam...
raphæ, vti, vti Vascus, Et L. Marineus Siculus perhibent. Anno. Christi, D CC XIIII. Saraceni Roderico vltimo Gothorum Rege, infausto octo dierum conflictu, vnuersa nobilitate deleta, totam Hispaniam partim vi, partim...
breuissimo tempore in potestate redigunt. Cantabris duntaxat, et Asturibus exceptis. Ac deinde, Anno D CC XV Dominica Palmar, Toletum fraude Iudæoru Mauris proditum fuit; Dum Christiani nihil minus suspicantes, ex...
audito verbo diuino. Ab eorum autem tyrannide liberatur et Christianæ Religioni restituitur, per Alfonsu Sextum, Anno. Dñi. Millesimo, nonagesimo tertio, vt ex Codice Alcobaciensi, et ex alio chronico, perantiquo, Vasæus not...

VALLISOLETVM, Alijs Pincia, cõmunter Valladolid dicitur, nobilisz.
totius Hispaniæ oppidum, Sereniss. Regis, Procerū, Illustriumq, virox, sedes est, ac proin magnificis ædificijs, tam nobiliū vsui, quàm cultui diuino
nitidissime constructis, præ cæteris Hispaniæ ciuitatibus superbisz. exornatur. Et ex opificum et mercator. frequentia, ex vbertate soli, ex
præterfluente pisuerga, haud contemnendas vtilitates percipit.

V M.

erexit fautore
alatium, a
litteris erat
prius, ferit
entential far
romißonibus
more vacarit

LLISOLETVM.

LEO

LEODII, Eburonum Augusta prima auspicia, in Ambiorigen magnanimum Eburonum Regem Hubertus Thomas Leodius refert,
eiusq; a casa Legione Romana in ea valle, ubi nunc est Leodium, Legia, nomen indicum constanter affirmat. Corrupto deinde vocabulo, Germanis Lut-
tich, alijs Leodium dicebatur. Vrbs est Germaniæ inferioris, quam et secundam vocant, maxima: ad tertiü a Tungris miliare, qua meridie spec-
tant, qua tanto murorum cingitur ambitu, ut altissimos complexetur montes vitibus pulcherrime consitos. Deinde in latissima excurrit, et appre-
hendit in valle planicie, in qua ex Arduenna sylua tria flumina Vta, Vesa, et Ambluaria in Mosam exonerant, et multas amœnissimas efficiüt in-
sulas, magnificis ædificijs exornatas, ita, ut ad voluptatè planè hic nihil desit. Exhibet hæc urbs octo insignia Canonicorū collegia, quatuor am-
plissimas abbatias, triginta duas ecclesias quas parrochiales vocãt, quatuor mendicantiü ordinü contubernia, et ex his nonnulla conduplicata, ut Fran-
ciscanorū. Quod si reliquas monachorū, et admirandarū monialium ædes, conuenticula, et sacella recensere velim, integro ferè libro opus esset, unde nö
mirum, si Franciscus Petrarcha scribat, se vidisse Leodium, insignè Clero locum. Habet ad meridie Arduennam sylua totius Galliæ maxima.
Ad alterū latus Tungros, et Centrones versus, est ager Hesbanicus, usq; adeo gleba fertili, adhæc pomis, et nucibus diis generis,
abundans, ut cum Sicilia de præstantia certare possit. Juxta ciuitatè effoditur nigri lapides, qui modico ligno accensi, calidissimü
ignein præbent. Aèr temperatissim est, et saluber. Mosa fluuio secatur per mediü, et pontib' arcuatis, solido cöstructis lapide con-
iungitur, ædificijs præstantissimis, et amplissimo Reuerēdissimi Palatio exornatur, cui si extremā manū addidisset artifices, ex sentētia Caroli
V. Imperatoris, in orbe Christiano nullū pulchrius futurū erat. Vrbs ipsa limpidissimis vrigat, fötibus; Jn qua tantū floruerūt litterarū
studia, ut uno tempore nouē ōs Regum; Ducum xx iiij. Comitū xxix. Baronū et ex prima nobilitate innumeri filij, apud Leodios
instituti legantur: Reuerendissimū Episcopum, tam in Ecclesiastica, quàm ciuili administratione dominū, et gubernatorem agnoscit.

DIVM. LIEGE

1. S. Laurent	17 S. Christofle	33 S. Ian Baptiste	49 S. Remÿ.
2. S. Gertruÿd	18 Les Frers Precheurs	34 S. George	50 Les Grieses seurs.
3. La Porte S. Martin	19 L'ospital S. Mathieu a la chaine	35 La Porte de Vinenigse	51 Les Frers des Carmes.
4. S. Martin	20 L'egliese S. Lambert cathedrale	36 La Porte S. Leonard	52 Les Frers Augustins.
5. La Porte S. Walburch	21 S. Andrieu	38 S. Foid. 39. S. Leonard.	53 Les Escoliers C. Reguliers.
6. S. Guilheaulme	22 Les Frers Mineurs	40 Le Baillair. ou maisõ pour	54 S. Phoÿn.
7. S. Babeline	23 Nre dame aux fons	Les infecteis de la peste	55 S. Nicolas.
8. S. Seuerin	24 S. Gengoulphe	41 Le pons des Arches	56 Le Pont S. Nicolas.
9. S. Hubert	25 Le Pons daueroit	42 S. Barbe	57 La Thour de Beche.
10. Le Pos fis des Beggars	26 S. Poul.	43 La Chambre des Abales friers	58 Les Frers Piedde schalz.
11. S. Croix	27 S. Martin en Isle	44 Les frers Fratres	59 Le Pont Damer court.
12. S. San Euangeliste	28 S. Denÿs	45 Les frers Croisters	60 S. Remacle.
13. S. Seruaes	29 S Estienne	46 Les Chainomes Reguliers	61 En Cornilloing.
14. S. Pierre	30 S Marie Magdalene	de Beaurepart	62 Les Frers Chaurtroux.
15. Le Pallais de Leuesq	31 S Catharine	47 La Tour a Comins.	63 Fornaise ou Lon fait le fer.
16. S. Adalbert	32 S Barthelmi	48 La Baye de S. Iaques.	64 S. Veronne.

VI

GANDAVVM, Amplißima Flandriæ orbs,
à Iulio Cæsare condita, et à suo nomine Caio, vt
Chronici Brabantini loquuntur, dicta, fluminibꝰ no:
bilis, amoena, apta, spaciosa, nunꝗ conclusa, riuisꝗ
suffocata. Innumeræ cultæꝗ domę, fæcunda viror, in:
genia, antiqui mores, cum duplici muro amplificata
loci species. Suos etia habet, vt Louaniu meditationi
ac studijs aptos receß. Habet et ludos litterarios ali:
quot multæ celebritatis, magnifica tępla, coeliꝗ quam
benigniu, genit frugale magis dixeris, ą parcu. Est Gã:
dauum et pluribꝰ sanctor, corporibꝰ et nobiliꝰ monaste:
rijs duobus exornatu, Petri Apostolorum principis, et
Bauonis. Vtrumꝗ Abbatem habet, ⁊ annuos prouę:
tus amplißimos. Carolo V. Aug. vita principium
dedit. Hadria: Barl.

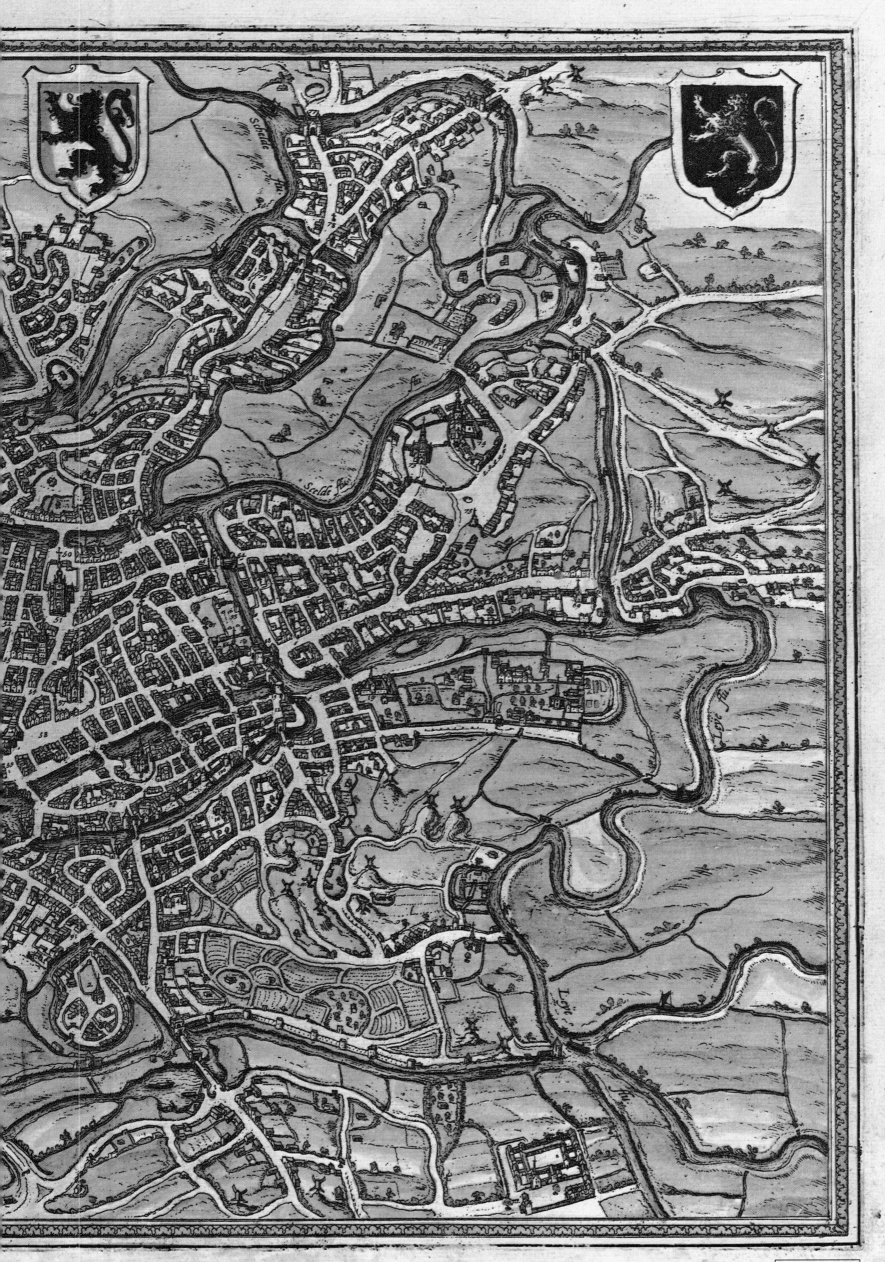

Schelde

Scelde flu:

Leye flu:

Leye

Porte de Bartemon

Minnebra

Porte de Mon

S.Walru

'S Gar

MONTES, HANNO-
NIÆ METROPOLIS.

S.

S. Niclas.

Porte Haure

Porte Nimi

Cum Priuilegio.

ATREBATVM, EPISCOPA:
LIS ET METROPOLI TI:
CA ARTESIÆ CIVITAS

Pierre Damant

Tholouse

1. Louensche poore
2. Couweberch poort
3. Oude Brussel poort
4. Anderlechtsche p.
5. Vlemsche poort
6. De Lake poort
7. Cuelsche poort
8. S. Lijsbet
9. S. Laureys.
10. S. Goele.
11. Baghijn Hof.
12. De Prekeren.
13. S. Loo.
14. S. Clarissen
15. S. Cornelis gasth:
16. Bekerde sonderss.
17. Couwenberch.
18. S. Madalena.
19. S. Claes.
20. Minderbrue.
21. S. Guerix.
22. Op de Sauele.
23. Vrouwebrues.
24. S. Iacops gasthj.
25. Fratres.
26. Swerte sust.
27. Ter Capellen.
28. Sellebrues.

29. Bogaerden
30. S. Geleijns gasthuys
31. S. Peter
32. S. Claren
33. Die warande
34. Veemart
35. Bergen
36. Regia
37. Die grote gulde hof
38. Cancelrije
39. S. Mertens kerchof
40. Hoochstraten
41. Atrecht
42. Die houtmart
43. Thof van Ludic
44. Den Werf
45. Aerschot
46. Nassue
47. Die Lombaerde
48. S. Ians gasthuys
49. Vischmart
50. Die groote mart
51. Stathuys
52. Die Oumart
53. Den Pant
54. Verloren cost
55. Gaesbeck
56. Egmont

S. Ian de mulebeke

Die Peerde
marst

Duersslach

Rosbemi

BRVXELLA, vrbs aulico-
rum frequentia, fontium copia,
magnificentia principalis aulæ,
Ciuicæ domus, ac plurium aliarũ
splendore, nobilissima: Et, quod de
sua Burdegala dixit Ausonius, clemẽ
tia hĩc cœli mitis, et irriguæ larga in
dulgentia terræ. Huius incolæ, vestitu
opes suas ostẽtant præ ceteris, et maxime genus mulierũ. Templorũ omnium
hõc loco magnificentiſsimum est
D. Gudulæ, Canonicorum Collegio
insigne. H.a: Barlandus.

IX

DEN AEM-
STEL.

Den Amstel

Le Proesse

Die Lastage

1. Clarissen.   15 S.Madalenen.
2. S.Joeris   16 S.Maergriete.
3. De Amstel.   17 S.Anghenuten.
4. Niewendonen.   18 S.Lisesen.
5. Oudendonen.   19 Houtmart.
6. Vij.Mach: 20 Die Plaets.
7. Paul.Broes.   21 Stathuys.
8. Die Raeme.   22 Oude kerck.
9. Beghijnhof.   23 Nieue kerck.
10. De Heiligerste. 24 Lievrowe kap:
11. S.Maria.   25 Tgasthuis
12. Claeren.   26 S Jakob kap:
13. Selle Broes.   27 Minnebroes
14. S.Barberen.   28 Selle susters.

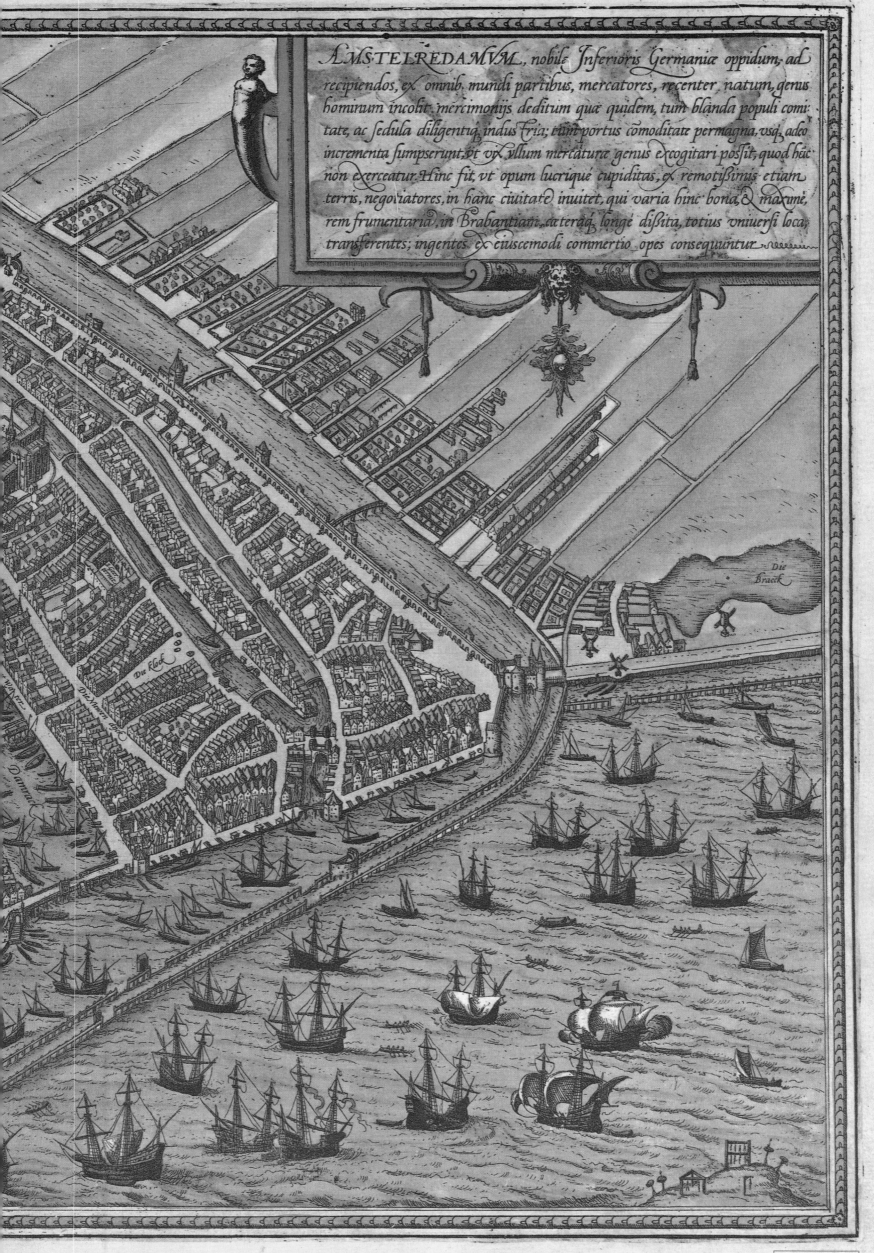

ALMSTELREDAMVM, nobile Inferioris Germaniæ oppidum, ad
recipiendos, ex omnib. mundi partibus, mercatores, recenter natum, genus
hominum incolit mercimonijs deditum qua quidem, tum blanda populi comi:
tate, ac sedula diligentiâ indus Fria; tum portus comoditate permagna, vsq; adeo
incrementa sumpserunt,vt vix vllum mercaturæ genus excogitari possit, quod hic
non exerceatur. Hinc fit vt opum lucrique cupiditas, ex remotissimis etiam
terris, negociatores, in hanc ciuitate inuitet, qui varia hinc bona, & maxime,
rem frumentaria, in Brabantiam, cæteraq; longe dissita, totius vniuersi loca,
transferentes; ingentes ex eiuscemodi commercio opes consequuntur

Die
Braeck

X

Den bemuerde werdt.

De Wor

Marten's Cat.

Bechleem Cl.

3 Cornelis capel.

Den Wech na ...

Vreeborch

TRAIECTVM CLARA ET VETVS EST EPISCOPALIS CIVITAS AN
TONINO MEMORATA, ITA DICTA, QVOD HIC ESSET TRAIECTVS VETERIS
RHENI, AVCTORE IACOBO MEYERO, IN ANNAL.LIB.FLAND.DICITVR AVTEM
TRAIECTVM INFERIVS, AD EIVS DIFFERENTIAM, CIVITATIS, QVAE EST
TRAIECTVM MOSAE, SEDES ALIQVANDO EPISCOPORVM TVNGRICORVM,
QVAE IAM EST LEODII. QVI PLVRA DE HAC VRBE DESIDERAT, IS
LEGAT AE.NEAM SYL: OTTONEM FRISIN: LIB.I.CAP:XV. VOLATER
RANVM, LIB:VII: ET LAMBERTI HORTENSII HISTORIAM.

HANC VRBEM ALII ATTRIBVVNT HOLLANDIÆ, ALII PHRISIÆ:
SIVE IN HOLLANDICO SOLO, SIVE IN PHRISIA SITA: HAVD DVBIO NO-
BILISSIMA EST ET PRIVATAR. ÆDIVM PVLCHRITVDINE ET CLERO.
HABET ENIM CELEBERRIMA CANONICOR. COLLEGIA IN QVIBVS PRINCI
PEM TENET LOCVM, QVOD EST D. MARTINI, HABET ET ANTISTITEM,
QVI IN SACRIS LATISSIME IMPERAT, HIC TAM DIVES AC POTENS,
VT SI QVANDO SIT NECESSE, QVADRAGINTA HOIVM MILLIA AD
BELLVM POSSIT ARMARE. HADRIANVS BARLANDVS.

ROTENBVRGVM ad Tubarum, elegans Franconiæ
oppidum, Hierosolomytanæ vrbi, situ respondere dicitur, à tur-
rium et tegular. rubore, nomen habens, olim proprijs ducibus
paruit. nunc imperio, post Friderici primi secula, accessit.

ROTEN

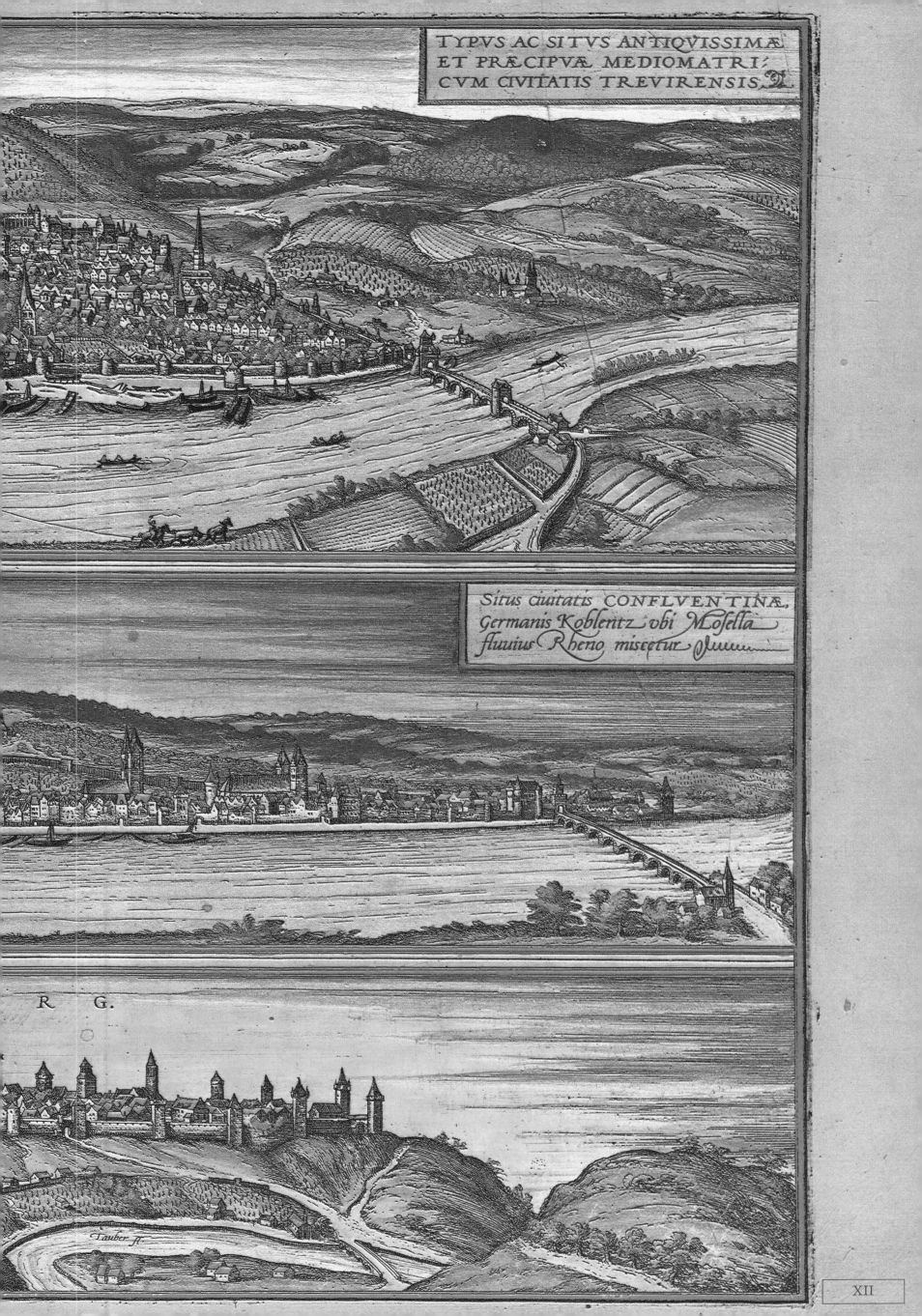

TYPVS AC SITVS ANTIQVISSIMAE
ET PRAECIPVAE MEDIOMATRI'
CVM CIVITATIS TREVIRENSIS.

Situs ciuitatis CONFLVENTINAE,
Germanis Koblentz vbi Mosella
fluuius Rheno miscetur.

R. G.

Tauber fc.

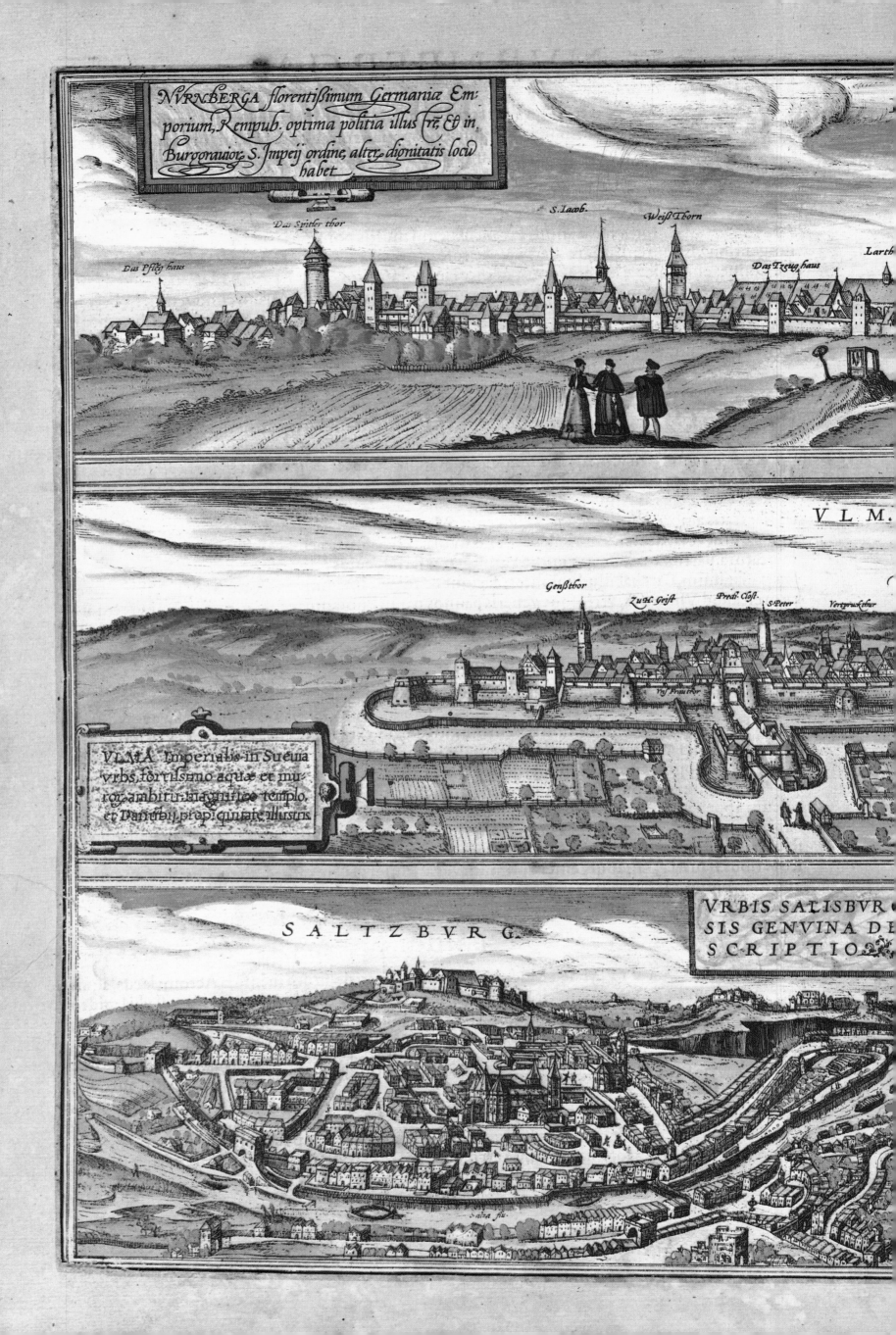

NVRNBERGA florentißimum Germaniæ Em:
porium, Renpub. optima politia illus trē, Et in
Burgorauior. S. Impeij ordine, alter dignitatis locū
habet

Das Pflēg haus   Das Spitler thor   S. Iacob.   Weiß Thorn   Das Tzeug haus   Larth

VLM.

Genßthor   Zu H. Geist   Predi Cloß.   S. Peter   Vertzpruckthur

VLMA Imperialis in Sueuia
vrbs, fortißimo aquæ et mu:
ror ambitu magnifico templo,
et Danubij propiquitate illustris

SALTZBVRG.   VRBIS SALISBVR
                              SIS GENVINA DE
                              SCRIPTIO

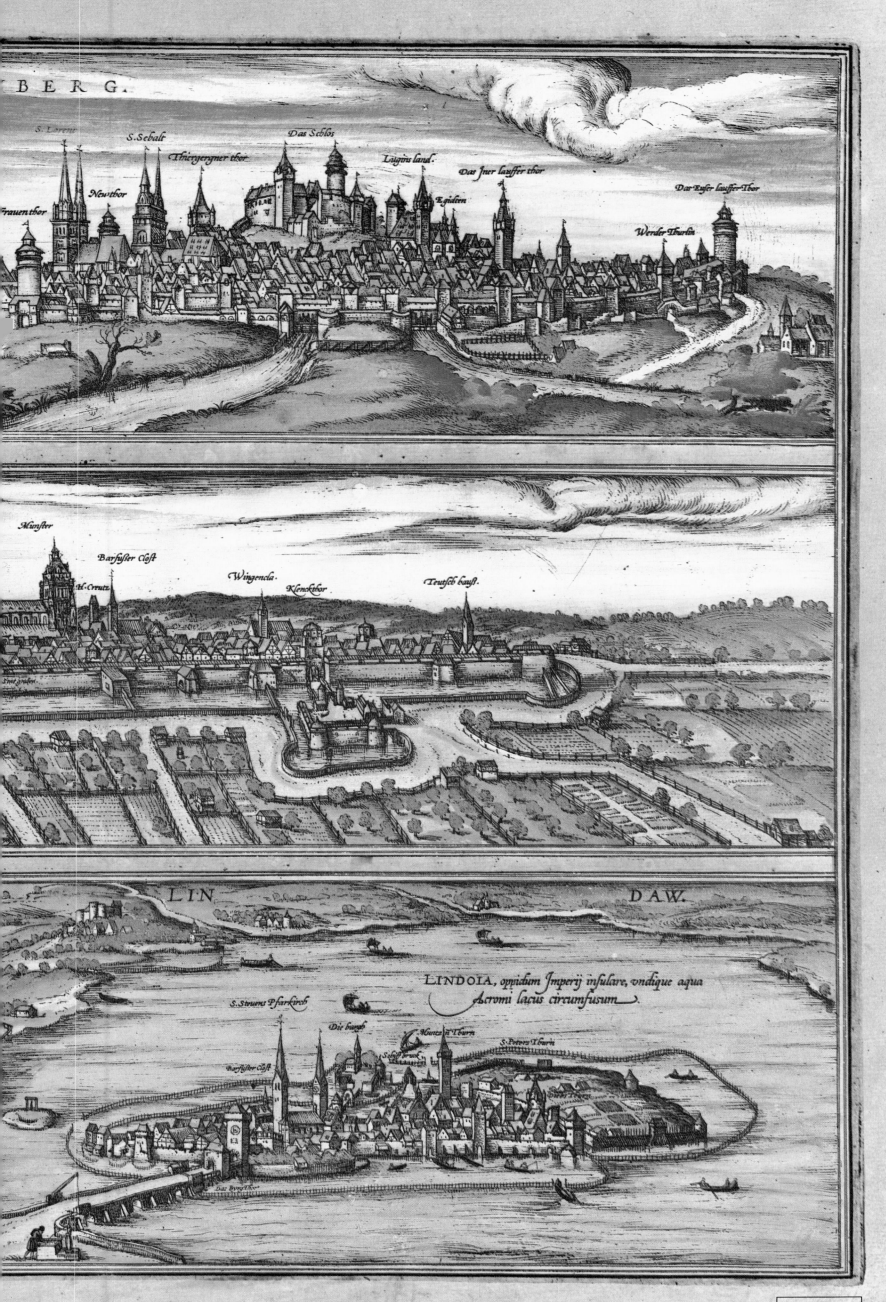

...BERG.

S. Lorens · S. Sebalt · Thiergertyner thor · Das Schlos · Lilgins land. · Das Jner lauffer thor · Das Euser lauffer Thor

Frauen thor · Newthor · Egidien · Werder Thurlin

Munster · Barfuser Clost · Wingencla. · Klenckthor · Teutsch hauß.

H. Creutz

LIN — DAW.

LINDOIA, oppidum Imperij insulare, vndique aqua
Acronii lacus circumfusum.

S. Struens Pfarkirch

Die burgh · Muntz n' Thurn · S. Peters Thurn

Barfuster Clost · Selos bruck

Das Byrg Thor

XIII

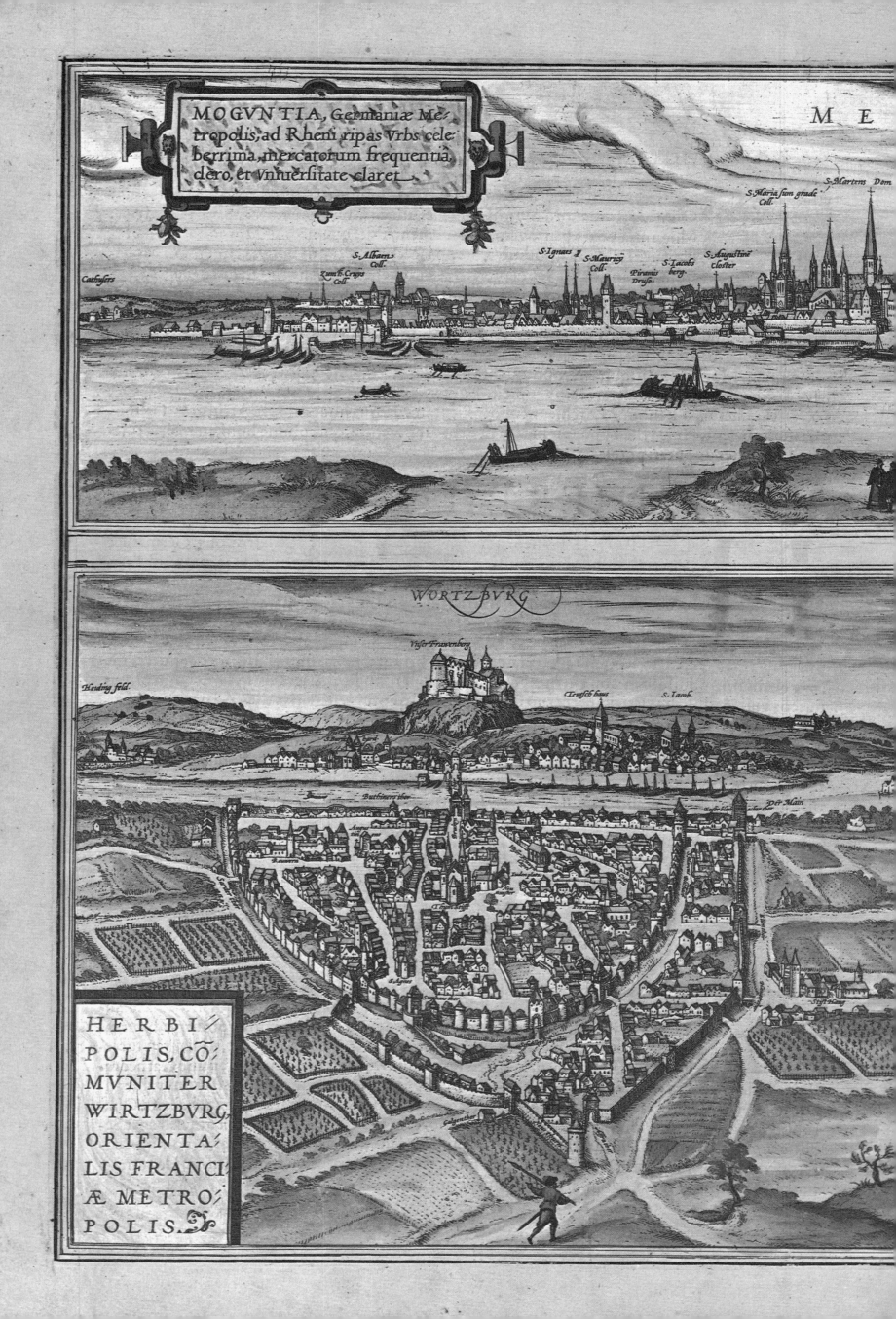

MOGVNTIA, Germaniæ Metropolis, ad Rheni ripas Vrbs celeberrima, mercatorum frequentiâ, clero, et Vniuersitate claret.

ME

Cathusers
Zum h. Crucs Coll.
S. Albans Coll.
S. Ignacs y
S. Mauricÿ Coll.
Piramis Druso.
S. Iacobs berg.
S. Augustinē closter
S. Maria sum grade Coll.
S. Martens Dom

WORTZBVRG

Vnser Frawenberg

Hending feld.
Treutsch haus
S. Iacob.
Buthiner thor
Der Main

HERBI-POLIS, CŌMVNITER WIRTZBVRG, ORIENTALIS FRANCIÆ METROPOLIS.

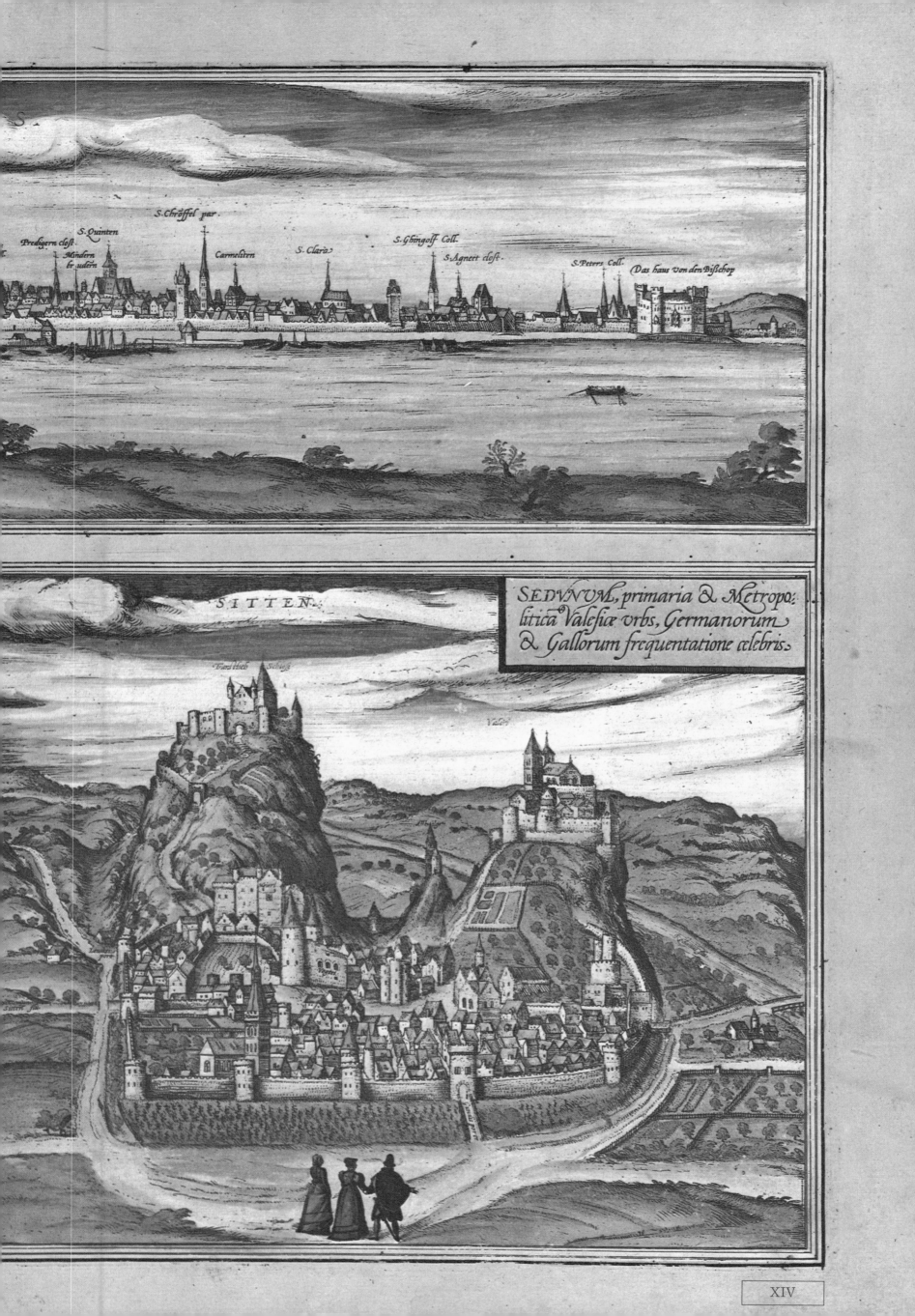

S.

Predigern clost. S.Quinten S.Chröffel par. Carmeliten S.Clara S.Ghingolf Coll. S.Peters Coll. Das haus von den Bißchop
Mindern bruder S.Agnect clost.

SITTEN.

SEDVNVM, primaria & Metropo:
litica Valesiæ vrbs, Germanorum
& Gallorum frequentatione celebris.

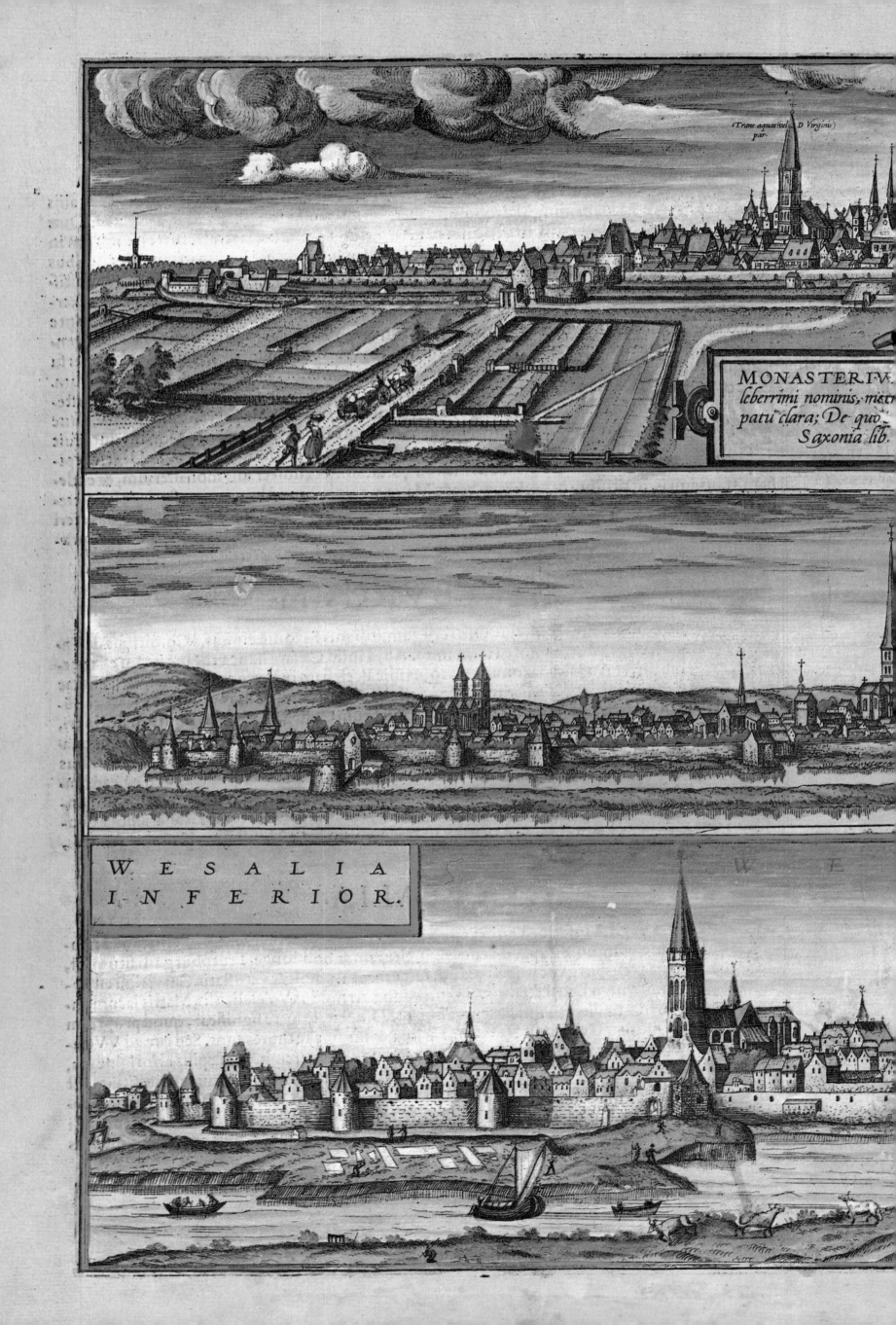

(Trans aquas vel D Virginis)
par.

MONASTERIV.
leberrimi nominis, mistri
patu clara; De quo
Saxonia lib.

WESALIA
INFERIOR.

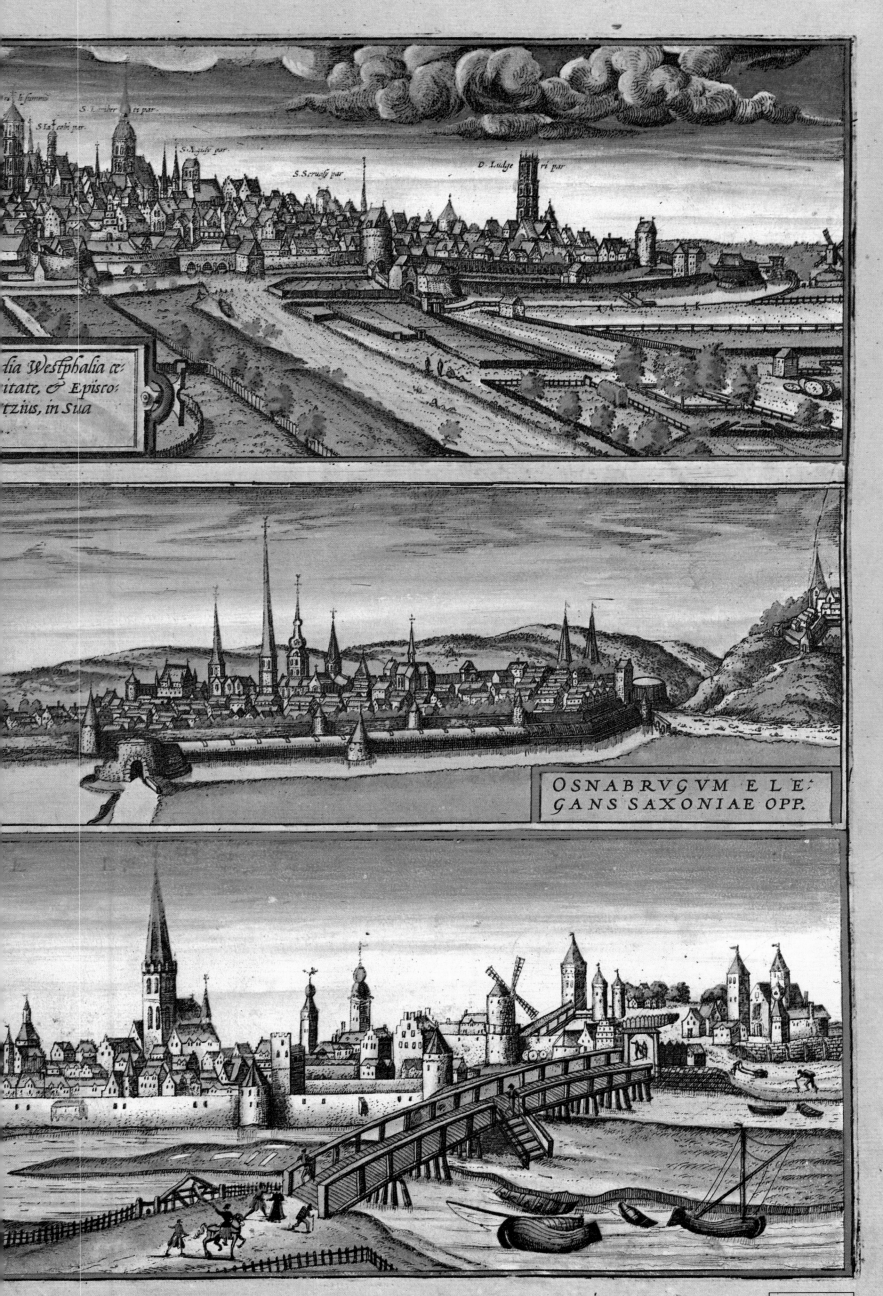

lia Westphalia cæ-
itate, & Episco-
tzius, in Sua

S. summis
S. Lamber ti par.
S. Iacobi par.
S. Ægidy par
S. Serufy par
D. Ludge ri par

OSNABRVGVM ELE-
GANS SAXONIAE OPP.

Dat Molen dor

De Dom

De oldest karck   S. Anna

S. Ti llien   Dat   Hoer
                     dor

S. Pet r

Dat R

LVBECA VRBS IMPERIAL
DALICARVM, ET INCLYT

HAMBVRG

S. Nicolaus

Der Heilig Geist
Miller dorff
Die Schaer kirch

S. Maria
Magdale

Die Nieder bruck

Hamburga, Florenti
æ emporium, Anglo
pore celeberrim

E. C.

Vnse Lefrowen karck S. Katrin S. Iac ob. S. Maria Magdalena TumHilge Geist S. Clemes Dat borch dor

...BERA, CIVITATVM WAN-
...NSEATICÆ SOCIETATIS CAPVT.

...ÉLICHE H...

Der T...buem Sanct Peter S. Iacob S. Gerdrut Das Stein To...
Joannes. Der Winser Port

...n inferioris Saxoni:
...equētatione hoc tē
...ni: M. D. LXXII.

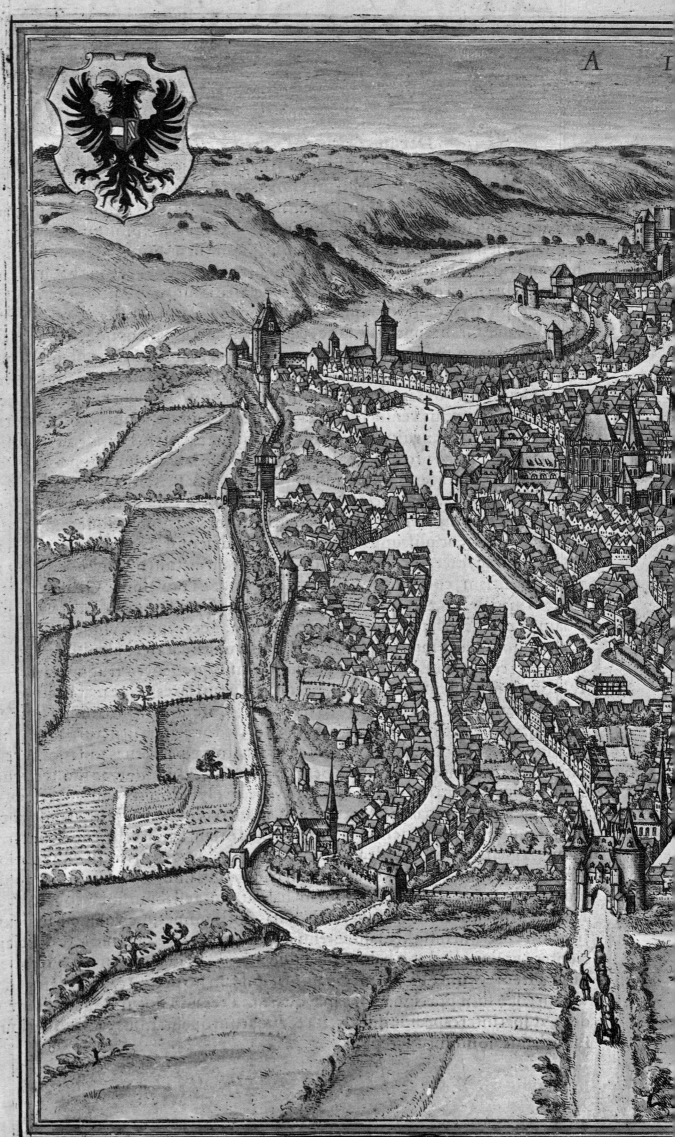

H.

AQVISGRA
NVM, VRBS PRÆ
CLARISSIMA
PRIMVM, INTER
QVATVOR IMPE
RII CIVITATES,
LOCVM OBTINET.

XVII

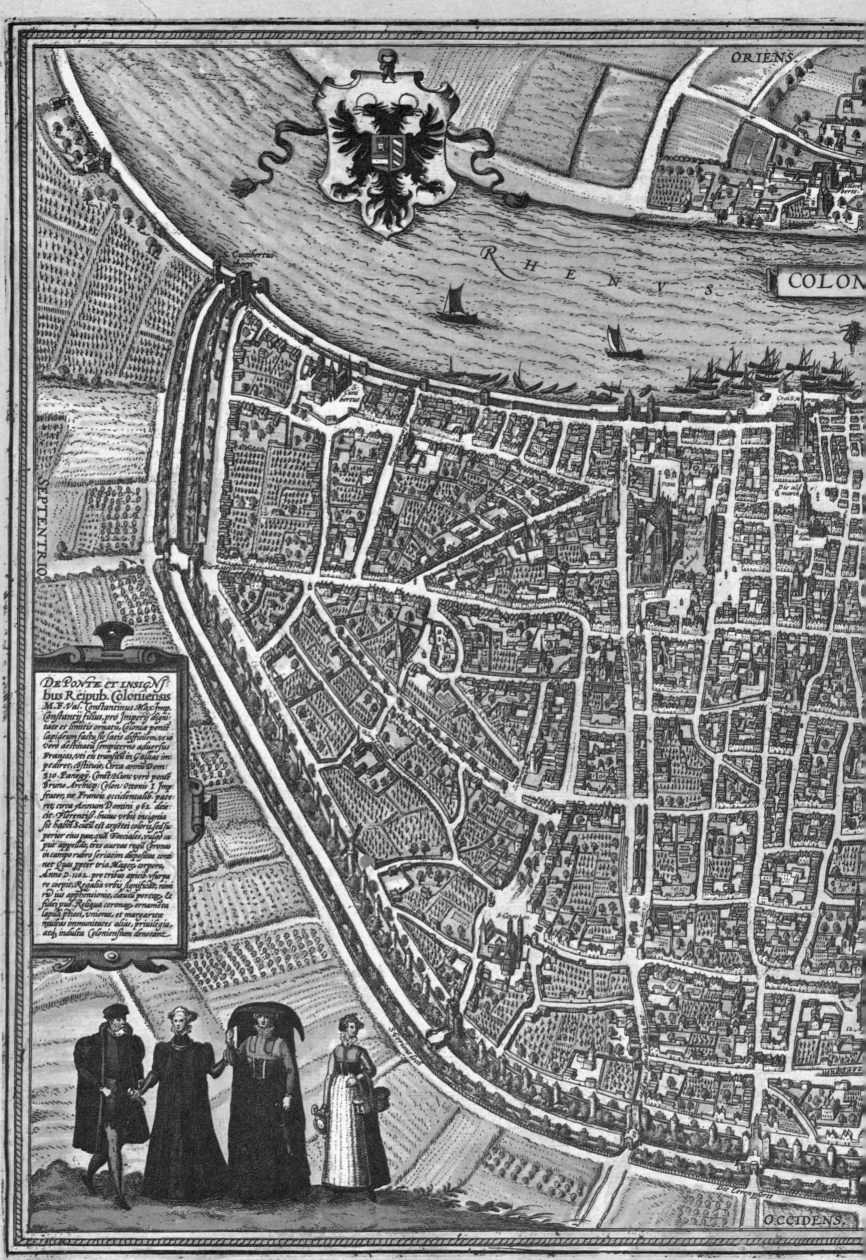

ORIENS

RHENVS

COLON

SEPTENTRIO

S. Cunibertus thom.

OCCIDENS

PINA. FLVVIVS.

MERIDIES.

Cum Privilegio.

DEVS RHENI.

XVIII

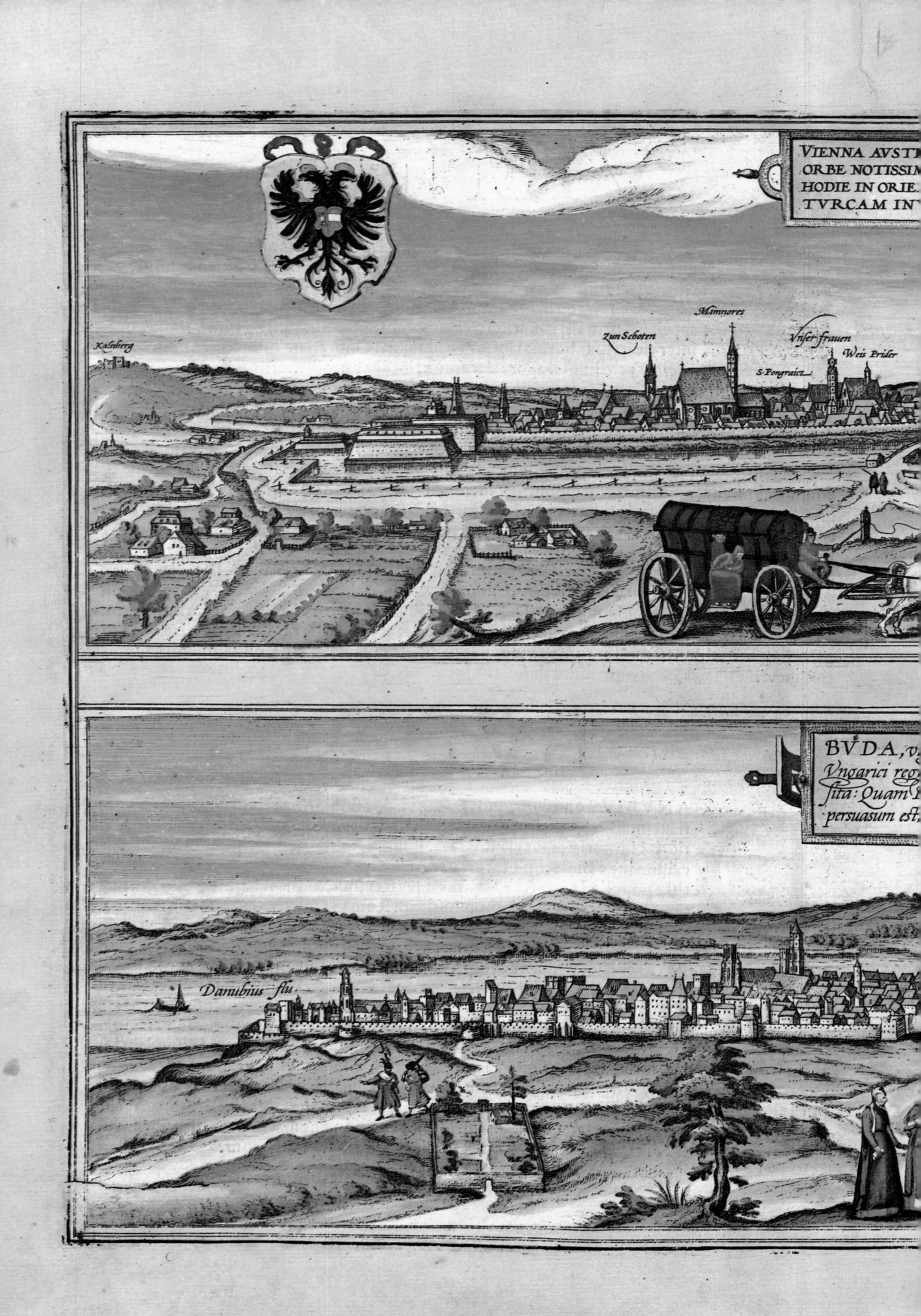

VIENNA AVST[...]
ORBE NOTISSIM[...]
HODIE IN ORIE[...]
TVRCAM IN[...]

Kalnberg

Zun Schoten

Mimnores

Vnser frauen

S. Pongraicz

Weis Prider

BVDA, v[...]
Vngarici regi[...]
sita: Quam [...]
persuasum est[...]

Danubius flu.

...POLIS, VRBS TOTO
...ISSIMAQ. VNICVM
...A SÆVISSIMVM
...OPVGNACVLVM.

S. Stteff and

S. Ecc

S. Augustins
S. Dorothea

Hemel Porten
S. Ieronimus.

S. Iohans.

S. Clara

...ima & regia
...Danubium
...rtam, vel, vt alijs
...aat. Fran: Ire:

Aula Regis

Catharina

Horti amœni

Aula marmorea

XIX

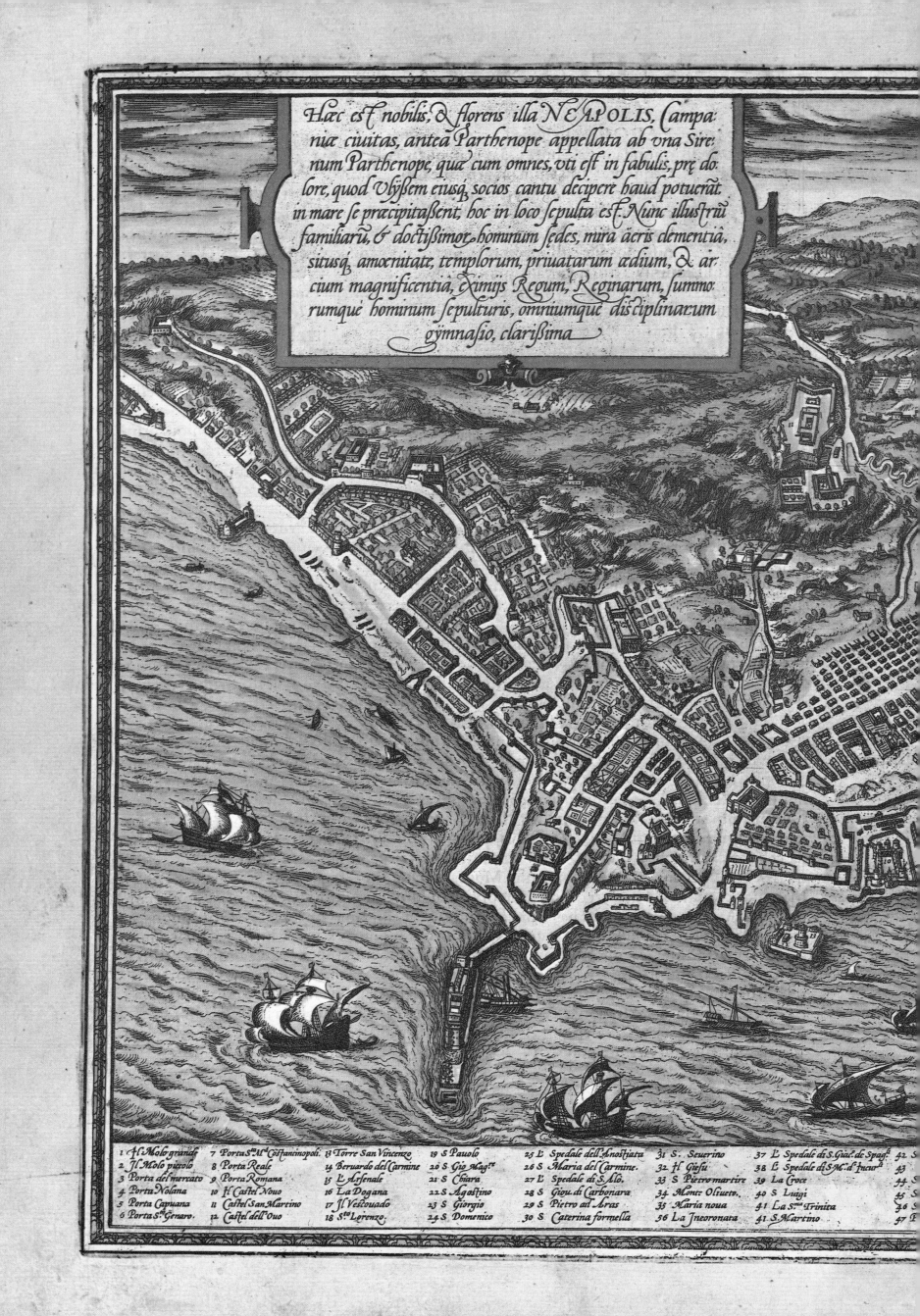

Hæc est nobilis, & florens illa NEAPOLIS, Campa-
nia ciuitas, antea Parthenope appellata ab vna Sire-
num Parthenope, quæ cum omnes, vti est in fabulis, prę do-
lore, quod Vlyßem eiusq̃, socios cantu decipere haud potuerũt,
in mare se præcipitaßent, hoc in loco sepulta est. Nunc illustriũ
familiarũ, & doctißimor. hominum sedes, mira aeris clementiâ,
situsq̃ amoenitate, templorum, priuatarum ædium, & ar-
cium magnificentiâ, eximijs Regum, Reginarum, summo-
rumque hominum sepulturis, omniumque disciplinarum
gÿmnasio, clarißima

1 Al Molo grande	7 Porta Sta Costantinopoli.	13 Torre San Vincenzo	19 S Pauolo	25 L Spedale dell Anõtiata	31 S. Seuerino	37 L Spedale di S. Giac. de Spag.
2 Il Molo piccolo	8 Porta Reale	14 Beruardo del Carmine	20 S Gio Magre	26 S Maria del Carmine.	32 Il Giesu	38 L Spedale di S M. d Incur.
3 Porta del mercato	9 Porta Romana	15 L Arsenale	21 S Chiara	27 L Spedale di S. Alo.	33 S Pietro martire	39 La Croce
4 Porta Nolana	10 Il Castel Nouo	16 La Dogana	22 S Agostino	28 S Giou di Carbonara	34 Montr Oliueto.	40 S Luigi
5 Porta Capuana	11 Castel San Martino	17 Il Vescouado	23 S Giorgio	29 S Pietro ad Aras	35 Maria noua	41 La Sta Trinita
6 Porta Sto Genaro.	12 Castel dell Ouo	18 Sto Lorenzo,	24 S Domenico	30 S Caterina formella	36 La Jncoronata	41 S Martino

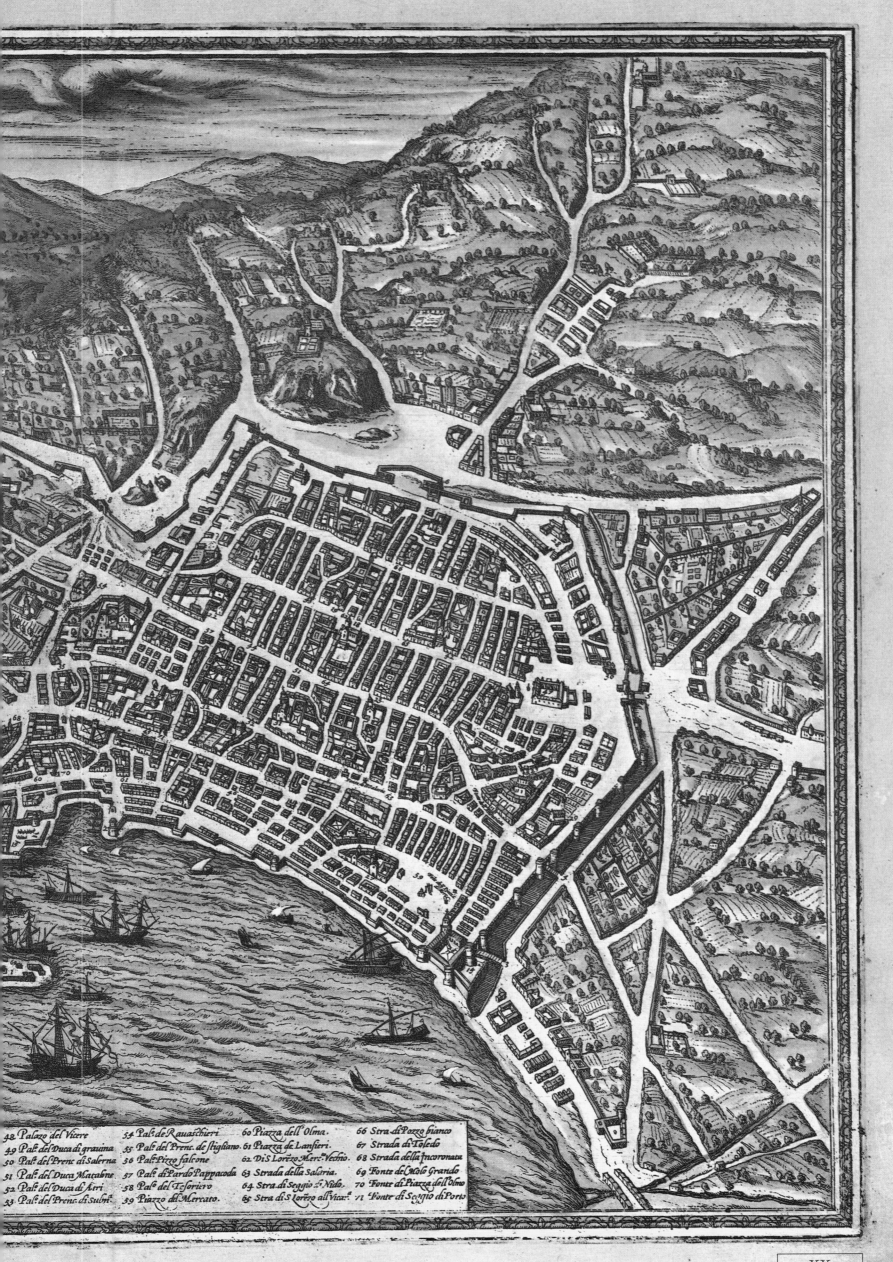

48 Palazo del Vicere   54 Palᵒ de Rauaschieri   60 Piazza dell'Olma.   66 Stra di Porzo bianco
49 Palᵒ del Duca di grauina   55 Palᵒ del Prenc. de stigliano 61 Piazza de Lanfieri.   67 Strada di Toledo
50 Palᵒ del Prenc di Salerna   56 Palᵒ Pizzo falcone   62 Di S Lorezo Merᵗᵒ Vechio 68 Strada della Incoronata
51 Palᵒ del Duca Matalone   57 Palᵒ di Pardo Pappacoda   63 Strada della Salaria.   69 Fonte del Molo Grando
52 Palᵒ del Duca di Arri   58 Palᵒ del Tesoriero   64 Stra di Seggio dᵒ Nido.   70 Fonte di Piazza dell'Olmo
53 Palᵒ del Prenc di Sulmᵒ   59 Piazzo del Mercato.   65 Stra di S Lorezo all'vicaᵃ 71 Fonte di Seggio di Porto

XX

153

S. Segondo frati

S. Maria monache

S. Giorgio dalega frati

S. Biasio catoldo monache

Igiesuati frati

S. Antolo de Concordia

S. Cosmo e damian frati

Canale de della Giudeca   La Croce monache

S. Gio Battista frati

La Giudeca

S. Clemente frati

Pouegia.

S. Spirito frati

Chioza Vescouado e podestaria

S. Maria da chioza

Malamocho Podestari

NOME DEIRII PRINCIPALI		
I Rio della Trinita	15 S. Marina preti	36 S. Samuello pti qui e un trag. che buta a san barnaba
II Dei Saloni	16 S. Maria noua preti	37 S. Barnaba pti
III Del Spirito santo	17 S. Cantiandone e il tragheto di mur. p.	38 S. Giouanne de rialto pti
IV De san Vio	18 S. Gio grifos como preti	39 S. Matthia de rialto preti
V De san Tronaso	19 S. Apost. pti qui e un trag. de rialto	40 S. Cassan preti
VI De san baseio	20 S. Sophia pti qui e il trag. che buta alla pescaria de rialto	41 S. Siluestro preti qui e un trag. che buta alla riua del carbi
VII De santa maria maggiore	21 S. Felixe pti qui e il trag. che buta alla calle [de i botteri]	42 S. Apponal preti
VIII Della croce	22 S. Fosca preti	43 S. Maria mater dol preti
IX Ric marin	23 S. Maria madalena preti qui e un tragheto che buta a san stia	44 S. Stai preti
X De san. giouanne decola	24 S. Marcuola preti qui e un trag. che buta al pal. del duca di ferrara	45 S. Giacomo dall orio p.
XI Della pergola	25 S. Lonardo preti	46 S. Giouan dcola preti
XII Dalle doi torre	26 S. Hieremia preti qui e un tragheto che buta a riua de biasio	47 S. Augustin preti
XIII De san cassan	27 Moise pti qui e un trag che buta alla trinita	48 S. Polo preti
XIV Della beccaria	28 S. Paterniano preti	49 S. Boldo preti
XV De san siluestro	29 S. Luca preti	50 S. Gieminiano preti
XVI De san madona	30 S. Frantin preti	51 S. Simeon grande preti
XVII De san polo	31 S. Benetto preti qui e un trag che buta a san polo	52 S. Stin preti
XVIII Della frasca	32 Anzolo preti	53 S. Simon picciolo preti
XIX Da cba foschari	33 S. Maria giubenigo pti qui e nu trag. cve buta a san gregorio	54 S. Pantalon pti doue sta il clariom...
XX Della mal paga	34 S. Maurino preti	Andrea loredan il qual a grã
XXI Di canareglo	35 S. Vidale pti qui e un trag che buta alla carita	qualita d'antiaglie de marmi bronzi et d'ogni sorte: meda
XXII De san marcola		glie che sono miracoloso da
XXIII De san felixe		vedere si che par es
XXIV De santo Apostolo		ser in un altra roma
XXV Del fontego di todeschi		
XXVI De san saluador		

XXVII Rio menudo
XXVIII Dall alboro
XXIX Rio menudo
XXX De palace
XXXI Dei schiaoni
XXXII Della pieta
XXXIII Dell arsenal
XXXIV De castello
XXXV De santo frepo

TVTTELE CONTRA DE OVERO
Parochie di Venetia
1 S. Piero da castello patriarcato
2 S. Biasio preti
3 S. Martin preti et anco hospedale
4 S. Giouanni in bragola preti
5 S. Antonin preti
6 S. Seuero preti iuridicion delle monache di san lorenzo
7 S. Prouolo preti iuridicio dele monache de san zaccaria
8 S. Trinita preti
9 S. Giouanne nuvo preti
10 S. Marco off. ila canonici del Ill. Sig.
11 S. Basso preti
12 S. Giulian preti et e Sula marzaria
13 S. Maria formosa preti
14 S. Lio preti

Corno Catedra
Corno Secretarij Cappella no Cussino
Serenissimus Venetorum Dux, cuius honor perpetuus, hoc habitu è es
praeferuntur octo ex serico, bina ex anea, totidem alba, ex vera...
et sax cum ense.

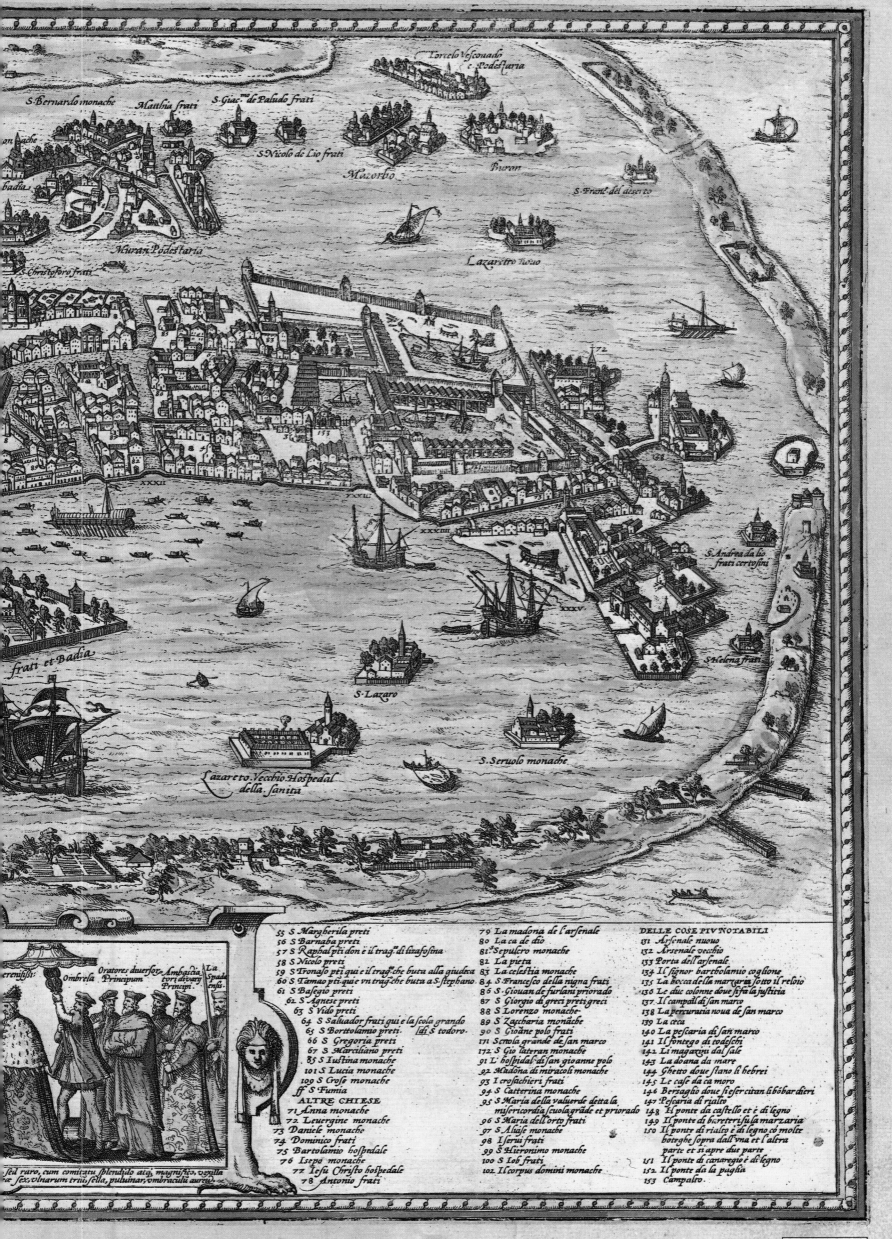

S. Bernardo monache   Matthia frati   S. Giac.mo de Paludo frati

S. Nicolo de Lio frati

Torcelo Vescouado e Podestaria

Mazorbo   Buran

S. Bernardo monache

S. Franc.co del deserto

Muran Podestaria

S. Christoforo frati

Lazaretto nouo

frati et Badia

S. Andrea da lio frati certosini

S. Lazaro

S. Helena frati

Lazaretto Vecchio Hospedal della sanita

S. Seruolo monache

Serenissi: Ombrela   Oratores duersor: Principum   Ambasciatori di vary Principi.   La Spada ensis.

sed raro, cum comitatu splendido atq, magnifico, vexilla sex, tubarum traisella, pulvinar, ombraculu aureu.

XXI

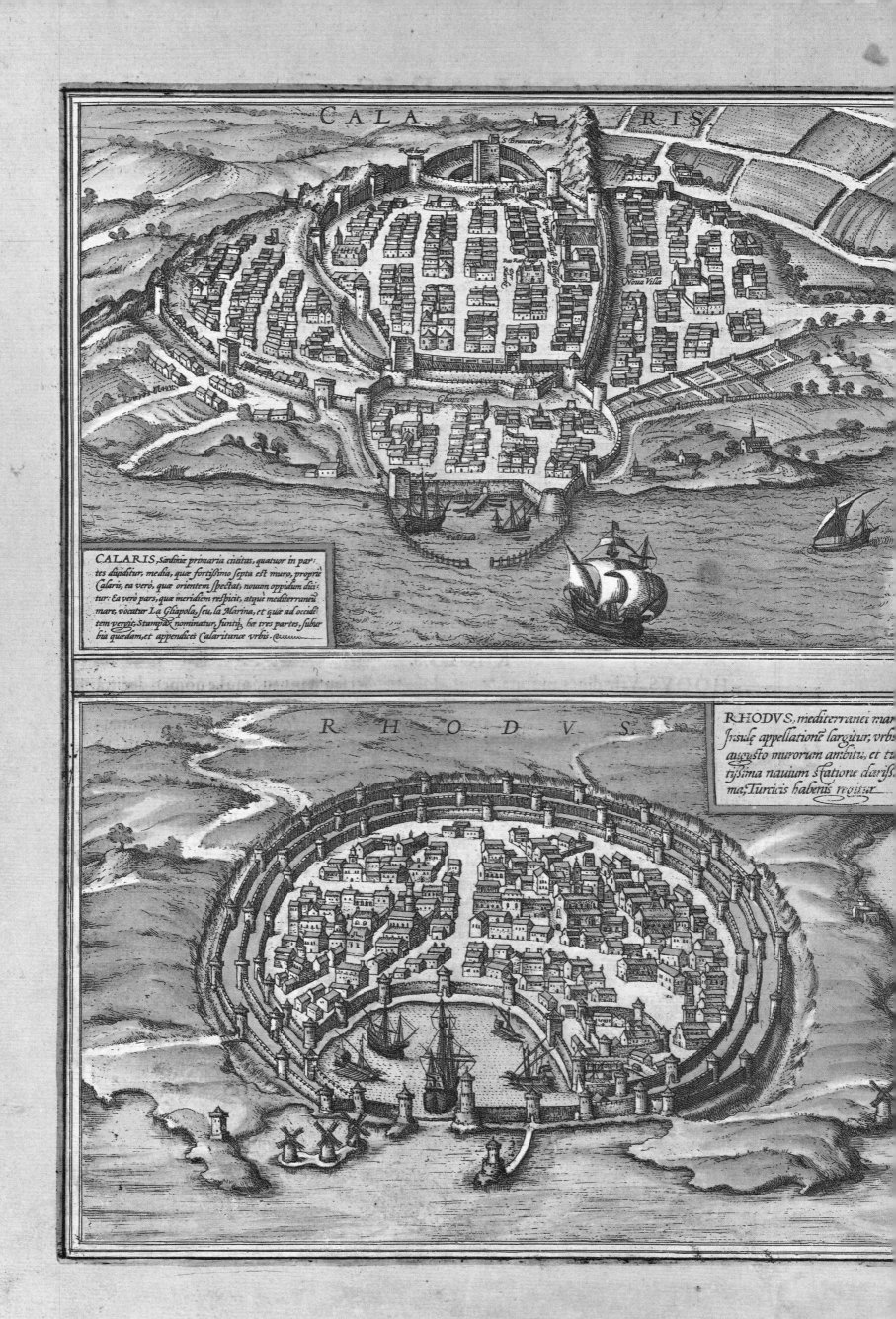

CALA RIS.

CALARIS, *Sardiniæ primaria ciuitas, quatuor in par:*
tes diuiditur, media, quæ fortissimo septa est muro, propriè
Calaris, ea verò, quæ orientem spectat, nouum oppidum dici:
tur: Ea verò pars, quæ meridiem respicit, atque mediterraneū
mare, vocatur La Gliapola, seu, la Marina, et quæ ad occidē:
tem vergit, Stampax nominatur, sintq; hæ tres partes, suburʒ
bia quædam, et appendices Calaritanæ vrbis.

R H O D V S.

RHODVS, *mediterranei mar:*
Insulę appellationē largitur, vrbs
augusto murorum ambitu, et tu:
tissima nauium statione clariss.
ma, Turcicis habenis regitur.

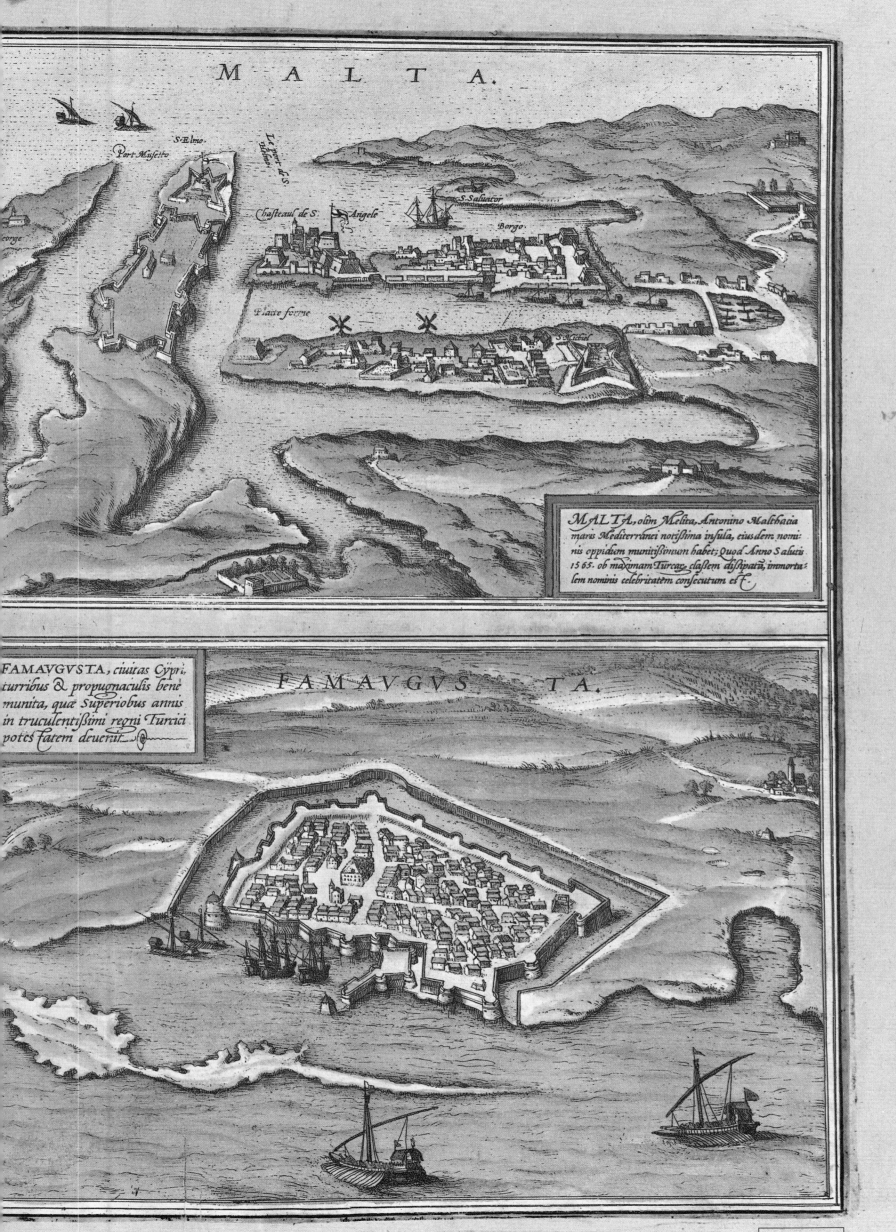

MALTA.

Port Muscito.

S. Elmo.

Le port de S. Hilarin.

Chasteaul de S. Angele

S. Saluator

Borgo

Place forme

S. Michel

MALTA, olim Melita, Antonino Malthatia maris Mediterranei notissima insula, eiusdem nominis oppidum munitissimum habet; Quod Anno Salutis 1565. ob maximam Turcar. classem dissipatā, immortalem nominis celebritatē consecutum est.

FAMAVGVSTA, ciuitas Cypri, turribus & propugnaculis bene munita, quæ superiobus annis in truculentissimi regni Turcici potestatem deuenit.

FAMAVGVS TA.

Hierosolyma, Clarissima totius Orientis ciuitas, Iudæ Metropolis, in duobus collibus, omnibus alijs in circuitu eminentioribus, sita fuit, qui colles duo, intermedia valle, habitationib. hominũ frequentiss. (quam Tyropoen vocat Iosephus, lib. 6. Bell. Iud. cap. 6.) separãtur Eminentior collis Sion dictus, in tres alios subdiuisus est. Primus is est, quem lib. 2. Reg. c. 5. Mello vocat, apud montẽ Giõn, In quo ædificatum erat antiquum Castrũ Siloe, quod occupabant Iebuseị, & à Dauide captum fuit, vbi idem quondam Arcam collocauit & sepulturæ locum elegit. Eodem hoc loco, constructũ cernitur Monasterium Franciscanoṛ, dictum Sion. Versus orientem verò, huius prædicti collis, alius adhuc erat qui ciuitas inferior dicebatur, in quo Palatium Dauid conditum fuit. Hunc locum inhabitauit idem, ante quam Iebusęorum castrum, quod in Mello erat, expugnasset. Ad Septentrionem verò, situs collis, Herodis Palatium habuit. Hi tres colles, vno murorum ambitu cincti, dicuntur ciuitas Dauid. Alter collis, duas partes habuit, vnam Montem Moream dictam, in quo Abraham obtulit filium suum Isaac, Ioseph: lib. 1. Antiq: c. 14. Quo in loco, postea Solomon templum cõstruxit, & in cliuo eiusdem montis, versus austrum, domum suã regiam, quã dicta fuit Palatium Solomonis. Hic collis, quia templũ habuit, etiam muro septus fuit, et ciuitati Dauid adiunctus Altera pars Acra cognominata, Moream versus, orientem contingens, cuius medietas vel pars vna Bezetha, hoc est, noua ciuitas dicta fuit, etiam muroṛ ambitu cincta, Huius Acræ medietas vel pars altera, contra torrentem Cedron posita, Palatium Assyriorum continet, fuitq, suburbium, moenib. clausum. Ita, vt prędicti quĩque colles, quaternis, ijsq, diuersis muroru cincturis conclusi fuerint &c. Hoc tempore Hierosolyma turcis Cuzumoharech dicitur.

Descriptio antiquæ vrbis Hierosolymorum, qua amplitudine et splendore tempore Christi Saluatoris nostri, conspicua fuit.

Noua vrbis Hierosolymitanæ descriptio, qua formâ
& situ nostro seculo se conspiciendam præbet.

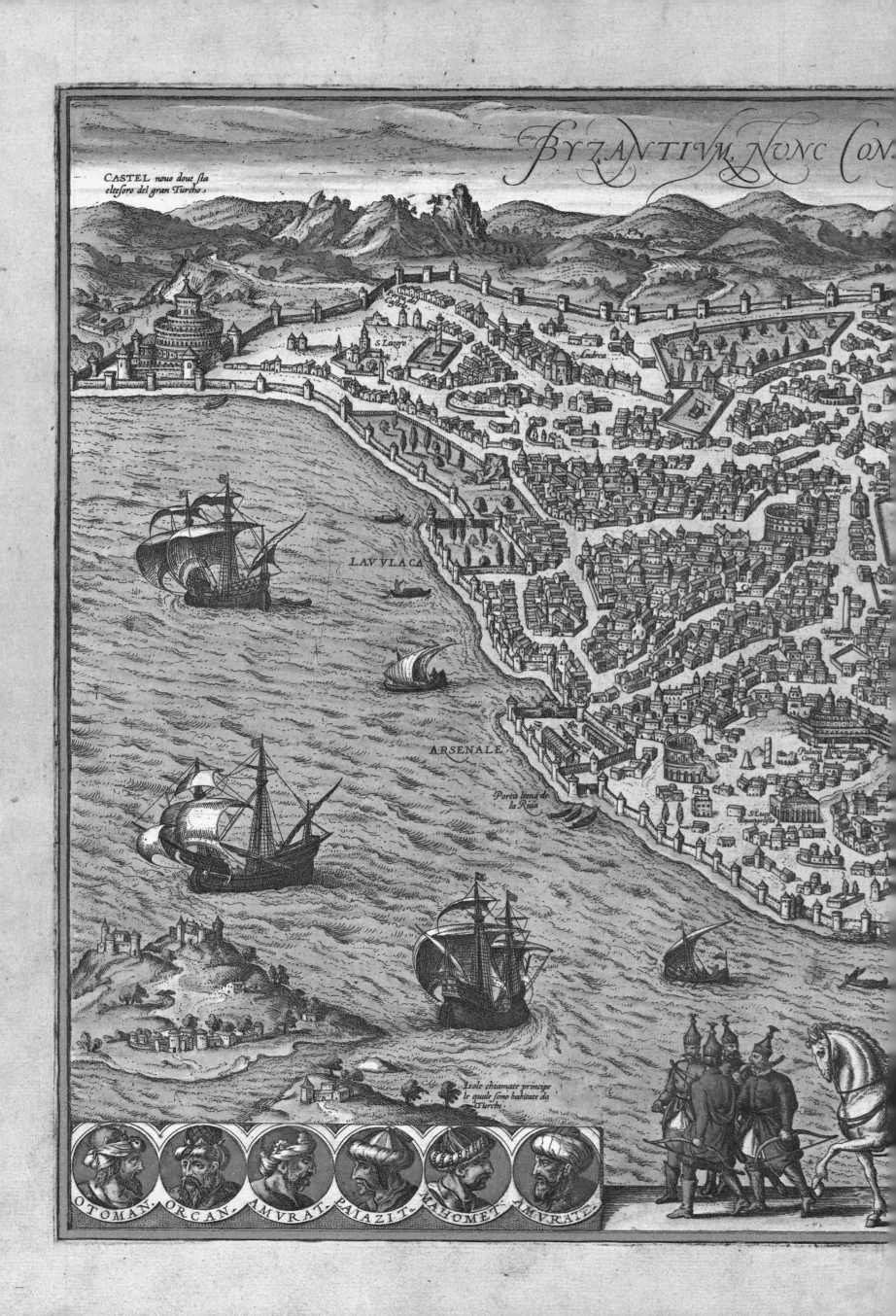

BYZANTIVM, NVNC CON

CASTEL *noue doue sta el tesoro del gran Turcho.*

S. Lazaro

Andrea

LAVVLACA

ARSENALE

Porta liona de la Riua

Asole chiamate principe le quale sono habitate da Turchi.

OTOMAN. ORCAN. AMVRAT. PAIAZIT. MAHOMET. AMVRATE.

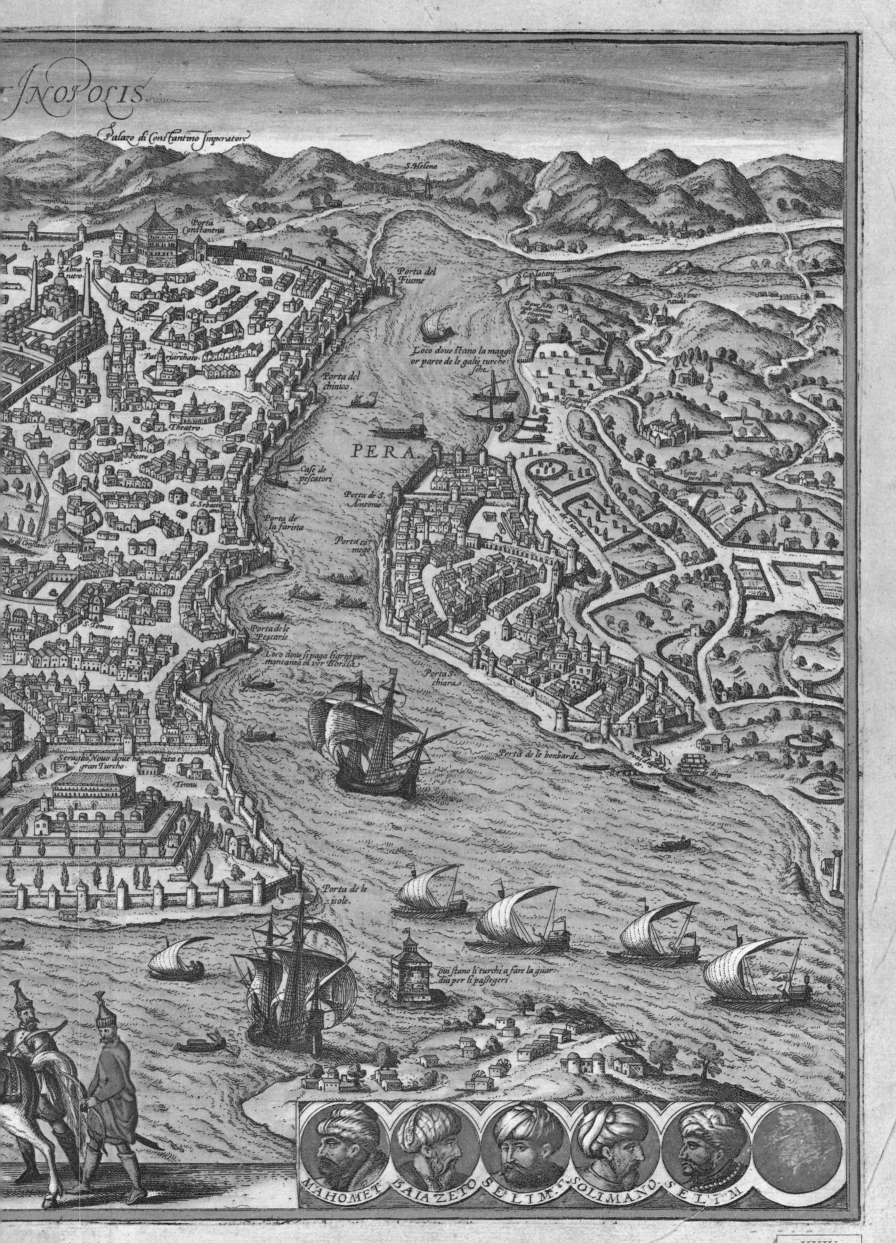

JNOPOLIS.

Palazo di Constantino Imperatore

S. Helena

Porta Constantia

Porta del Fiume

Galatan

S. Vene ratilia

Porta del chinto.

Loco doue stano la maggi or parte de le galie turche sche

Case de pescatori

PERA

Porta de S. Antonia

Vigne persi di

Porta de la farina

Porta co mtego

Porta de le Pescarie

Loco doue si paga il carso per montanea in ver Borsia.

Porta S. chiara

Porta de le bonbarde

Serugho Nouo doue ha bita el gran Turcho

Porta de le isole.

Qui stano l'turchi a fare la guar dia per li passegeri.

MAHOMET *BAIAZETO* *SELIM.* *SOLIMANO* *SELIM*

Crocodili

Dactili

Arena

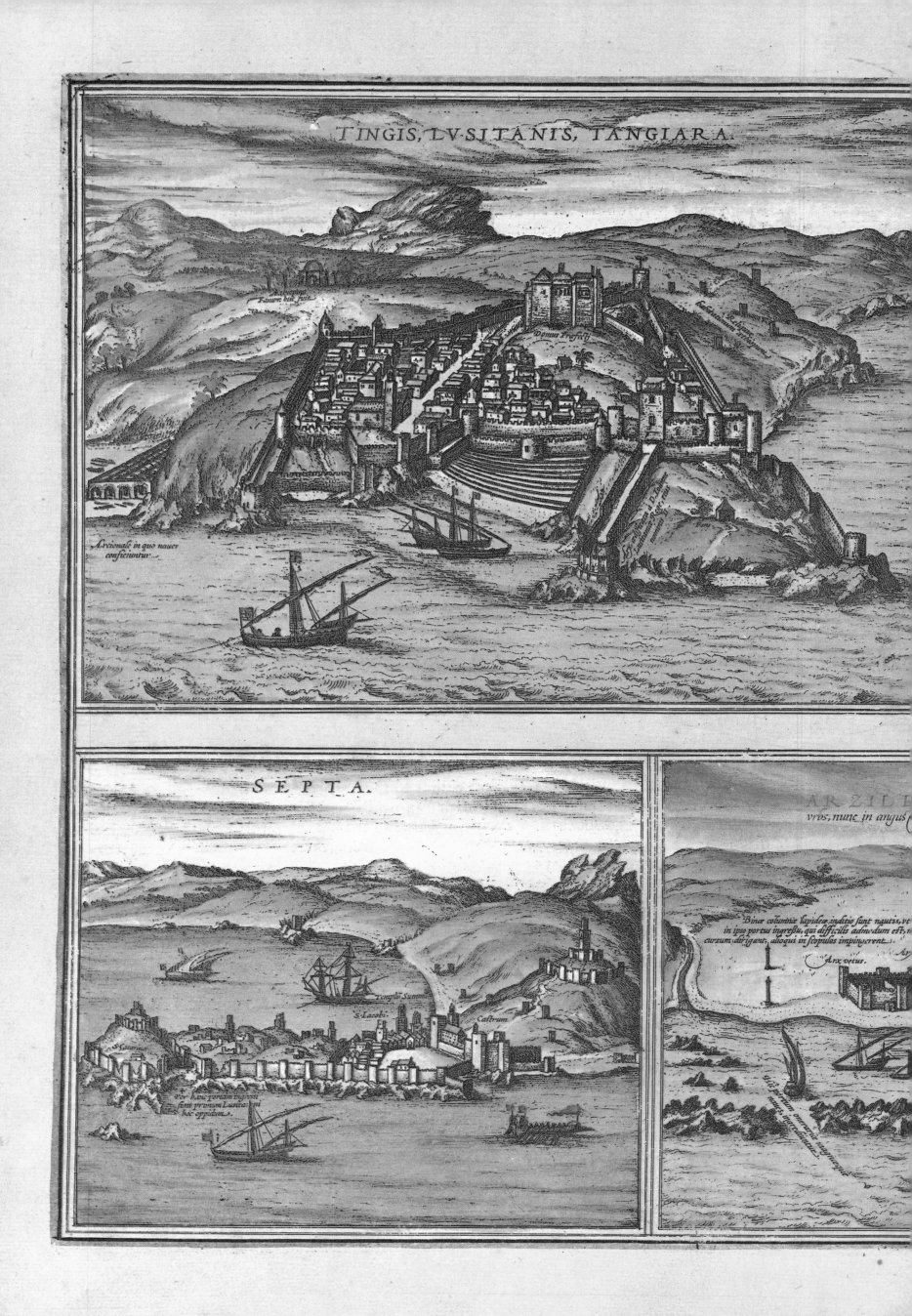

TINGIS, LVSITANIS, TANGIARA.

SEPTA.

ARZIL
vrbs, nunc in anguſ

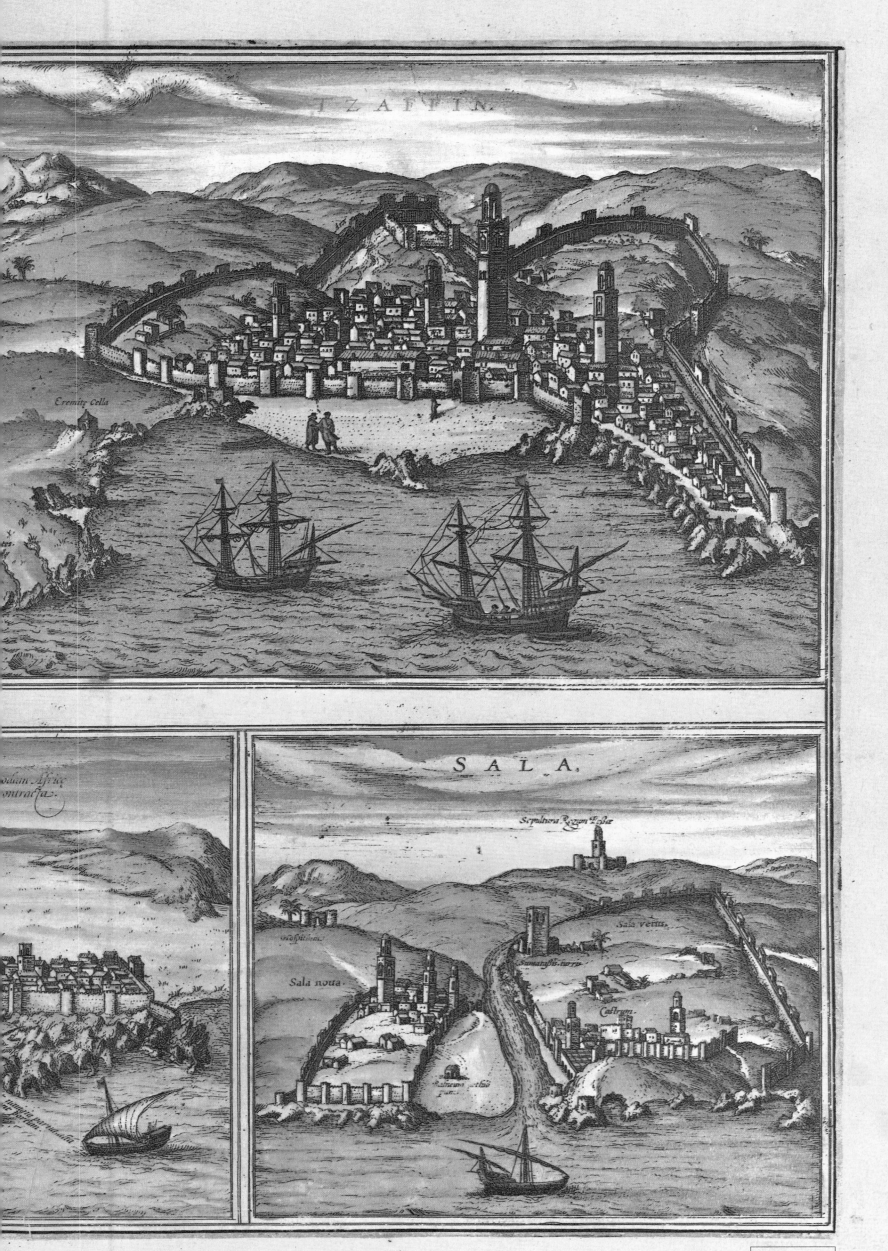

SAFFIN

SALA.

XXVI

MOMBAZA

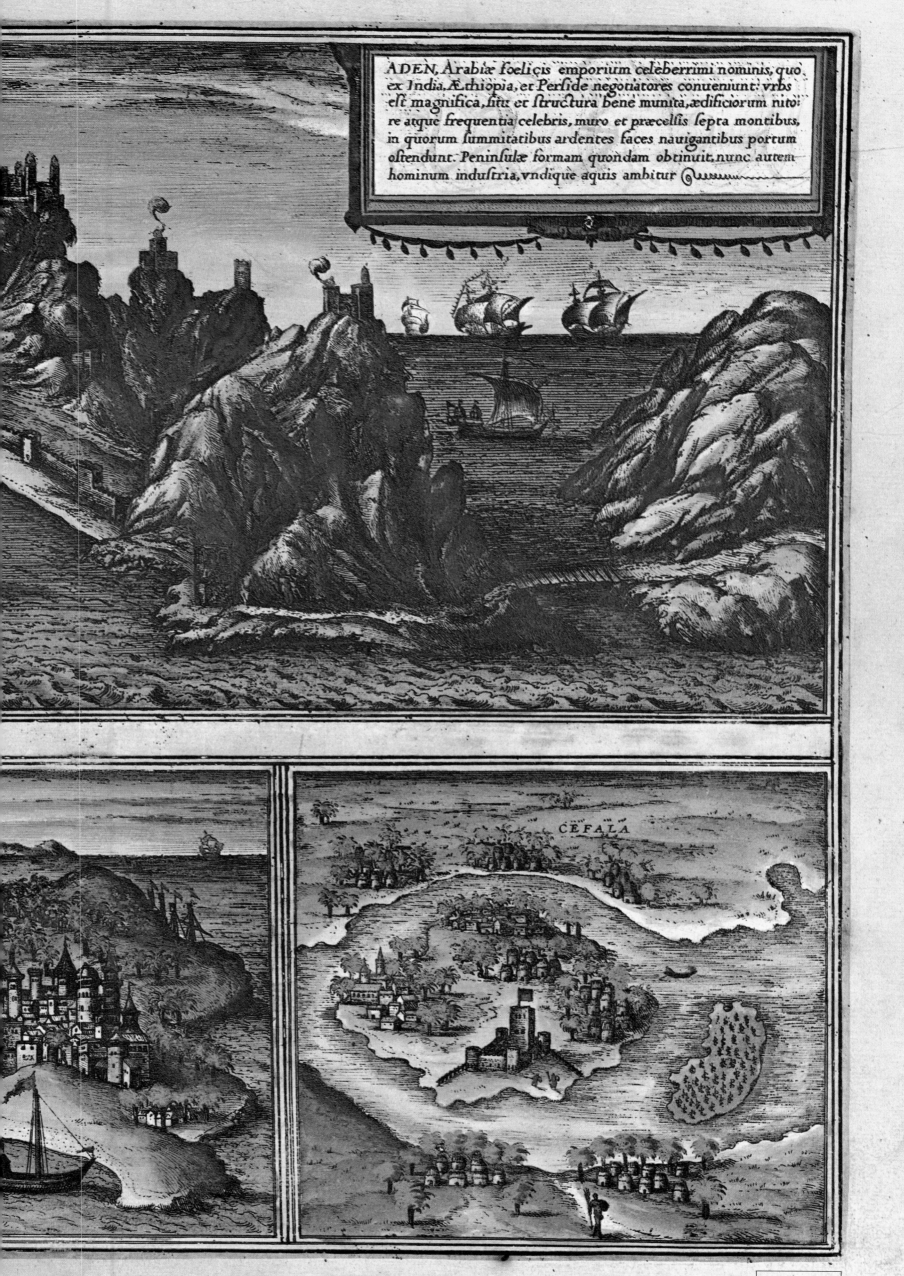

ADEN, Arabiæ foeliçis emporium celeberrimi nominis, quo
ex India, Æthiopia, et Perside negotiatores conueniunt: vrbs
est magnifica, situ et structura bene munita, ædificiorum nito:
re atque frequentia celebris, muro et præcelsis septa montibus,
in quorum summitatibus ardentes faces nauigantibus portum
ostendunt. Peninsulæ formam quondam obtinuit, nunc autem
hominum industria, vndique aquis ambitur

CEFALA

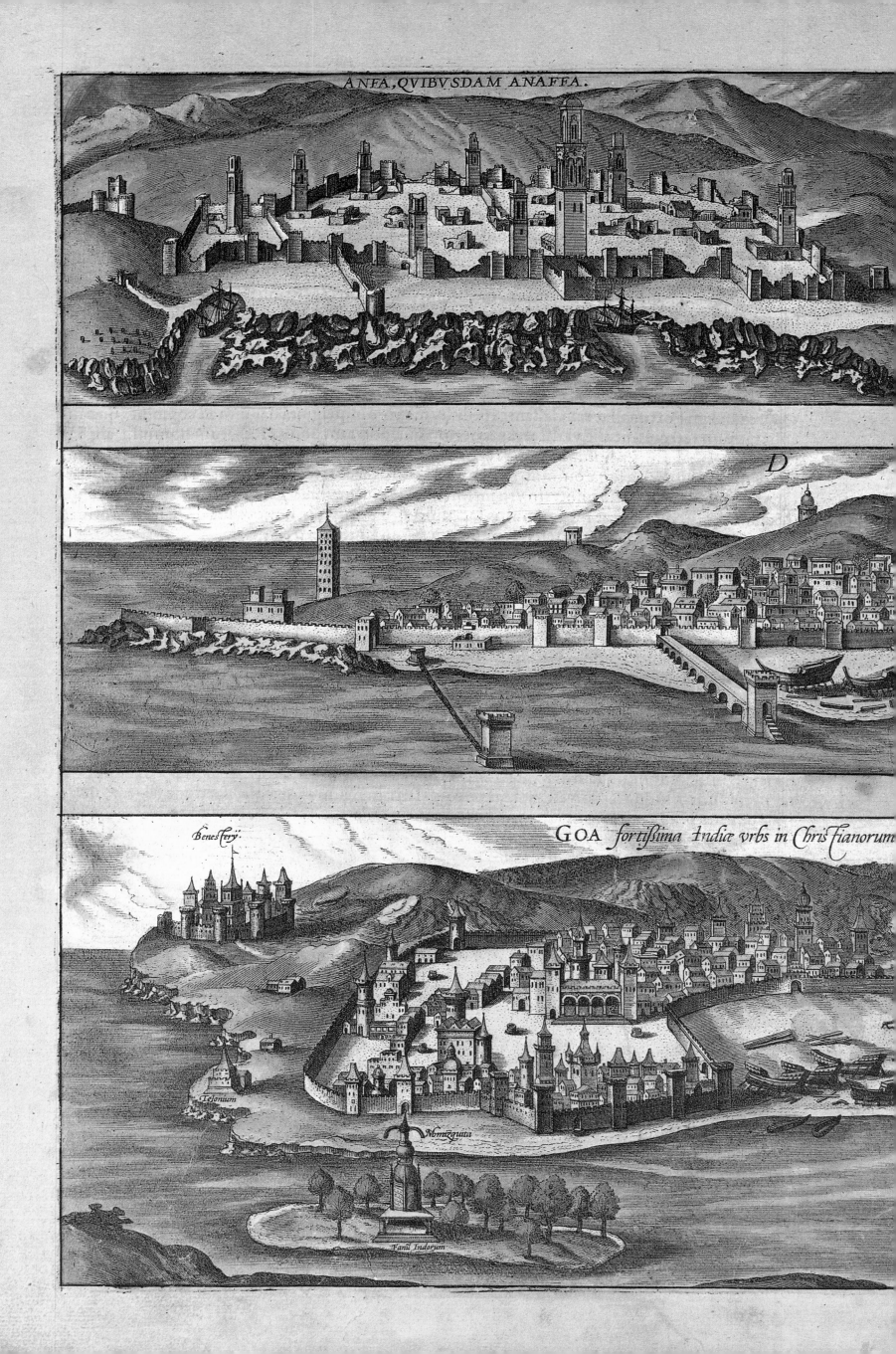

ANFA, QVIBVSDAM ANAFFA.

D

Benes fery.

GOA fortissima Indiæ vrbs in Christianorum

Telonium

Mvirzquita

Fanü Indorum

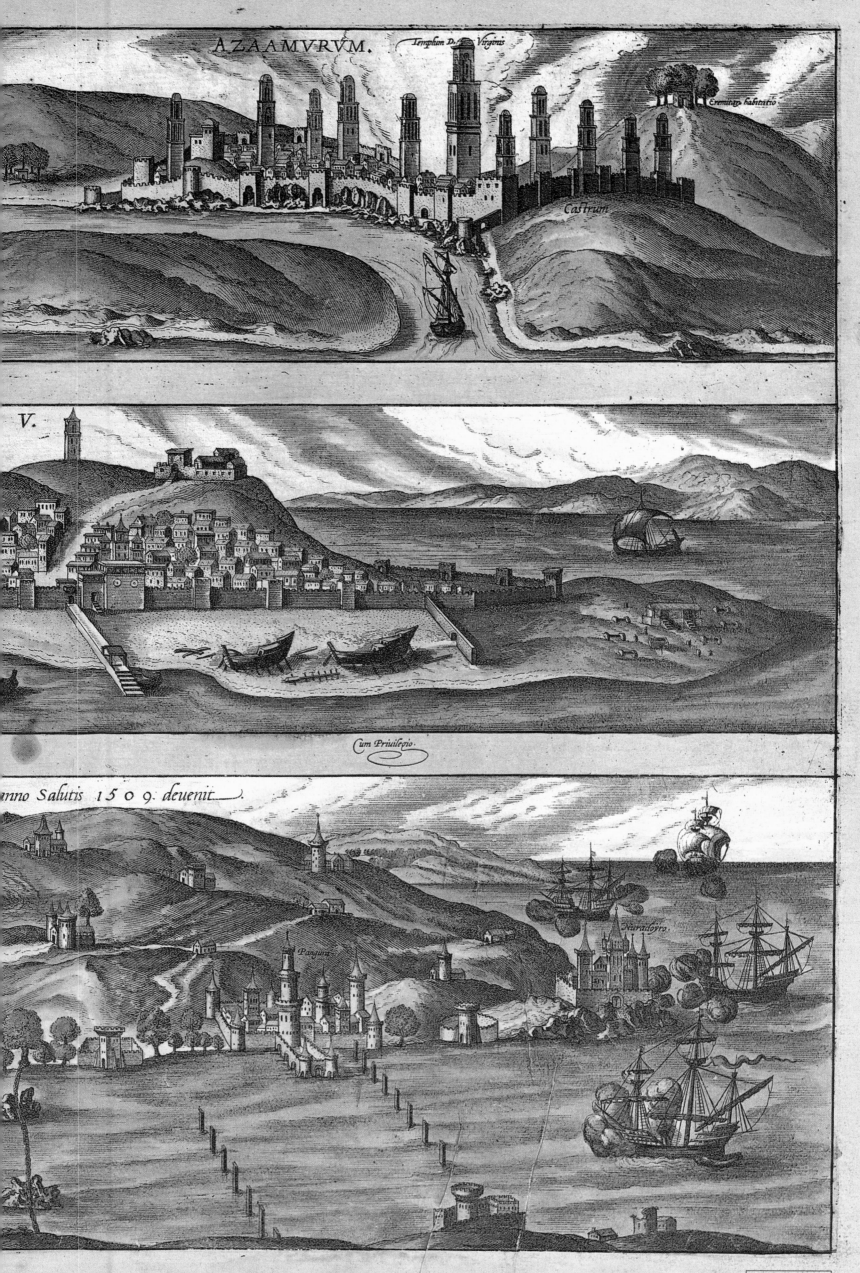

AZAAMVRVM.

Templum D. Virginis

Eremitæ habitatio

Castrum

V.

Cum Privilegio.

anno Salutis 1509. devenit.

Castrum

Naradoyro.

Pangum

XXVIII

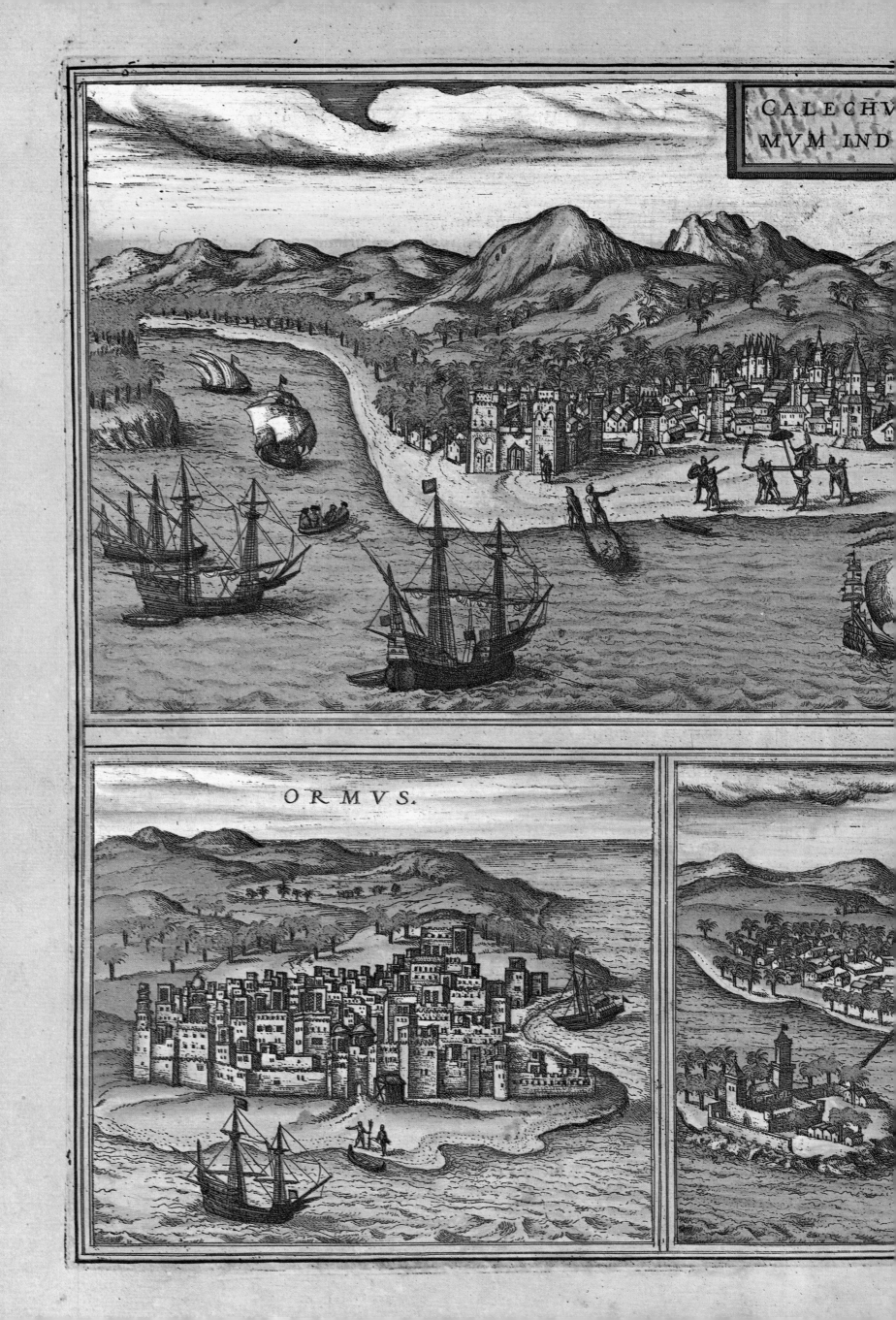

CALECHV
MVM IND

ORMVS.

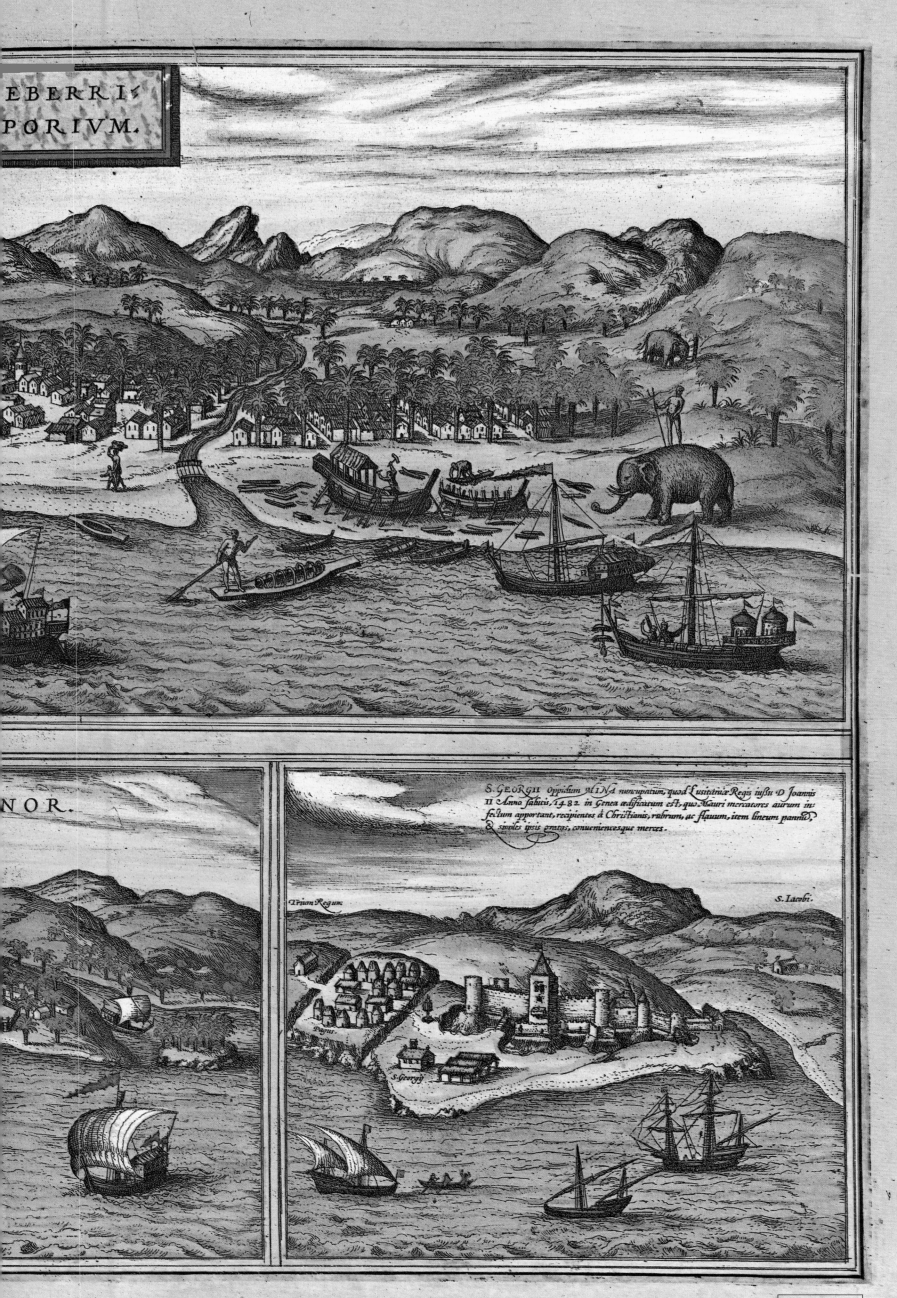

EBERRI: PORIVM.

NOR.

S. GEORGII *Oppidum MINA nuncupatum, quod Lusitania Regis iussu D Joannis II Anno salutis, 1482. in Genea adificatum est, quo Mauri mercatores aurum insectum apportant, recipientes à Christianis, rubrum, ac flauum, item lineum pannu, & similes quisis emtas, conueniencesque merces.*

Trium Regum.

S. Iacobi.

Pagus.

S. Georgÿ

12.45 5-96